Cambridge Elements

Elements in American Politics
edited by
Frances E. Lee
Princeton University

COOPERATING FACTIONS

A Network Analysis of Party Divisions in U.S. Presidential Nominations

Rachel M. Blum
University of Oklahoma

Hans C. Noel
Georgetown University

Shaftesbury Road, Cambridge CB2 8EA, United Kingdom

One Liberty Plaza, 20th Floor, New York, NY 10006, USA

477 Williamstown Road, Port Melbourne, VIC 3207, Australia

314–321, 3rd Floor, Plot 3, Splendor Forum, Jasola District Centre,
New Delhi – 110025, India

103 Penang Road, #05–06/07, Visioncrest Commercial, Singapore 238467

Cambridge University Press is part of Cambridge University Press & Assessment,
a department of the University of Cambridge.

We share the University's mission to contribute to society through the pursuit of
education, learning and research at the highest international levels of excellence.

www.cambridge.org
Information on this title: www.cambridge.org/9781009495608

DOI: 10.1017/9781009495615

When citing this work, please include a reference to the DOI 10.1017/9781009495615

First published 2024

A catalogue record for this publication is available from the British Library

ISBN 978-1-009-49560-8 Hardback
ISBN 978-1-009-49563-9 Paperback
ISSN 2515-1606 (online)
ISSN 2515-1592 (print)

Cooperating Factions

A Network Analysis of Party Divisions in U.S. Presidential Nominations

Elements in American Politics

DOI: 10.1017/9781009495615
First published online: November 2024

Rachel M. Blum
University of Oklahoma

Hans C. Noel
Georgetown University

Author for correspondence: Rachel M. Blum, rblum@ou.edu

Abstract: Popular accounts of presidential nomination politics in the United States focus on factions, lanes, or even a civil war within the party. This Element uses data on party leader endorsements in nominations to identify a network of party actors and the apparent long-standing divisions within each party. The authors find that there are divisions, but they do not generally map to the competing camps described by most observers. Instead, they find parties that, while regularly divided, generally tend to have a dominant, establishment group, which combines the interests of many factions, even as some factions sometimes challenge that establishment. This pattern fits a conception of factions as focused on reshaping the party, but not necessarily on undermining it.

This Element also has a video abstract: www.cambridge.org/EAMP_Blum

Keywords: political parties, political networks, factions, presidential nominations, coalitions

ISBNs: 9781009495608 (HB), 9781009495639 (PB), 9781009495615 (OC)
ISSNs: 2515-1606 (online), 2515-1592 (print)

Contents

1 Presidential Nominations in Intra-party Conflict

After the first few contests in 2020, the Democratic presidential primaries were shaping up to be a messy rerun of the fight in 2016, in which "establishment" candidate Hillary Clinton held off a challenge from party "outsider" Bernie Sanders, a progressive who viewed most of the Democratic Party as too moderate.

By the 2020 South Carolina primaries, Sanders had finished first or second in Iowa, New Hampshire, and Nevada, and enjoyed a surge in national polling. It seemed that he might be in the lead. Unlike in 2016, the "establishment" wing of the party did not have a single clear champion. Pete Buttigieg had beaten or tied Sanders in Iowa and New Hampshire, but Joe Biden and Amy Klobuchar also won significant numbers of votes. It seemed possible that the more unified progressive wing of the party could exploit the fragmented support for the more moderate candidates.

Then, at the end of February, a decisive Biden win in South Carolina convinced Klobuchar and Buttigieg to drop out of the race, throwing their support to Biden. Many other prominent Democrats also announced support for Biden. Now, it was the progressives who seemed divided, with Elizabeth Warren possibly drawing support from the same pool of voters who might favor Sanders. Biden went on to win big on Super Tuesday and clinched the nomination soon after.

This narrative of the 2020 nomination race is the conventional wisdom (e.g. Korecki and Siders 2020; Korecki 2020; Bacon 2020; Allen and Parnes 2021) of what happened. It incorporates several key points most observers have made about the process.

First, the competition among candidates is viewed as competition among well-defined factions in the party – "progressives" against the "establishment." While these factions might ebb and flow, the implication is that they persist over at least the medium term, covering several election cycles. Such factions also exist in the Republican Party, where party "regulars" have faced challenges from a group of procedural radicals, known by names such as the Tea Party and Make America Great Again (MAGA).

Second, each faction is thought to need one champion. If more than one candidate is running within a faction's "lane," those candidates will split the faction's support, letting the other side win. Donald Trump's outsider challenge to the Republicans in 2016 was successful because the anti-Trump forces were so fragmented, while Clinton dispatched Sanders much more easily in that year because the anti-Sanders vote was not spread out among other establishment candidates.

Finally, the factions in the presidential nomination fight are seen as a reflection of divisions in the party more broadly. A progressive wing exists in Congress, so of course it will manifest in nominations.

All three of these observations, and this general narrative, have much truth to them. Political parties are coalitions, and coalitions have fault lines. Those fault lines should be especially visible in nomination contests, which by their very nature pit different members of the same party against each other.

But we argue that much is missing from this picture.

Parties are coalitions, but *intra*-party coalition politics is not merely *inter*-party politics replicated inside the party. Parties, particularly party leaders, have a strong incentive to try to hold their coalitions together. Those incentives are especially powerful for presidential nominations, which designate the effective leader of the entire party. The weight of this choice changes the strategies of party coalition members in ways that this narrative does not account for.

1.1 Factions and Nominations

The choice of a presidential candidate is a particularly illuminating place to look for how parties manage their factions. Political parties are, in E.E. Schattschneider's (1942) words, "a maneuver in numbers" (p. 38) in which potentially distinctive politicians, perhaps representing differing factions, coordinate for victory. Parties perform this task in every arena, from the legislature to the electorate. But, according to Schattschneider, nominating candidates might be "the most important activity of the party" (p. 64).

In choosing a leader, parties need to identify one person who can represent all their factions. Many politicians can succeed as agents of their own factions. But leaders, especially the president, must try to appeal to everyone.

Our central argument is that this changes how both the party establishment and any competing factions will approach the presidential nomination. The result is a mixture of cooperation and conflict.

Factions can try to cooperate with the mainstream of the party, influencing their choices, while ultimately accepting a compromise. Or they can try to win over the nomination by brute force. Establishment politicians similarly can try to co-opt rival factions, or they can try to block them out altogether.

These two strategies – cooperation or conflict – are both likely present for every nomination. Which prevails depends at least in part on the institutions that the party has for selecting a nominee. As Nelson Polsby (1983) argued, the post-reform institutions of the U.S. parties do not adequately provide the "coalition forcing" mechanism that would ensure that cooperation dominates. In that institutional environment, both strategies should be present, but it is an empirical question which ones dominate.

In fact, these two strategies are central to the distinction between the establishment and other factions. Observers typically use the word "establishment" to refer to the dominant or in-power group, but also to those who are the traditional and usually more moderate or pragmatic part of the party. Our focus will be on the first sense. The esablishment is the part of the party that is running things, and other factions might challenge it.

1.2 Networks

We look for evidence of these strategies in the presidential nomination behavior of party leaders.

In every nomination contest, party notables express their support for different possible nominees. Previous research has shown that these endorsements are at least predictive of (Steger 2007), and perhaps influential on (Cohen et al. 2008) the outcome of the contest.

We look at these data from a different perspective. If party leaders believe that their endorsements will be helpful to their supported candidate, what can we learn from studying who supports whom?

For each party, we trace out the network of support among these party elites. Did the politicians who supported Hillary Clinton in 2016 go on to support Joe Biden in 2020? Did the Reagan people in 1980 become the Bush people in 1988?

Social Network Analysis (SNA) allows us to describe these networks of support and identify the subcommunities within them. This in turn will give us a richer insight into the factional tendencies of the parties.

Presidential endorsements are, on the one hand, a natural place to look for factional behavior. But, as we will argue, they are also far from ideal. Because politicians are being strategic, their endorsements will not always reveal their true internal preferences. This is true of most political behavior, and especially of elite political behavior.

This is both a weakness and a strength of our approach. The data we have will not reveal every factional cleavage, only those that extend to behavior. So we may not be able to map the actual factions. What we are mapping is the extent to which those factions shape nomination politics. If the incentives to factionalize dominate, we will find factions. If the incentives to cooperate dominate, we will find unity. To the extent that both are present, we will find evidence of both.

And we do find both. By looking systematically across a long period of time, we find evidence of factional behavior. We also find still more evidence of repeated efforts to find a compromise.

1.3 Section Outline

The coming sections present a focused investigation into these questions in the specific context of recent presidential nominations.

In Section 2, we systematically explore what a faction is, and how they might show up in presidential nomination politics. A faction is not just any subgroup within a party, but one that aims to change the direction of the party from within. Even if factions are present, they may coordinate and compromise with others in a nomination contest.

Section 3 turns to our data and methods. We extend the data set on presidential endorsements from Cohen et al. to include data from 2012 to 2020. We supplement the resulting data set, which includes all presidential nominations for a major party candidate from 1972 to 2020, with biographical information on each endorser. In this section, we explain the application of SNA methods to this data set and provide readers with an overview of the networks in the two parties.

Section 4 takes an in-depth look at the divisions within the parties. We use a network-based clustering approach known as community detection to identify the groups of endorsers who tend to make the same decisions together over time. These are *communities* and are central to our analysis. By bringing in a variety of biographical and political characteristics of the endorsers within the communities, we can characterize each community. This method detects four communities in the Democratic network, and ten in the Republican network (only six of which are large enough to analyze). The communities in each party are split between the establishment and possible factions.

Section 5 returns to the narrative we introduced at the beginning of this section, and especially to the idea of "lanes" in presidential nominations. Using our data and survey data of primary voters, we demonstrate that presidential nominations are less about lanes and more about building consensus among factions.

Section 6 maps our network communities onto factional caucuses in the U.S. House. We examine whether our factional communities correspond with distinct patterns of factional caucus membership. These data also allow us to probe the possibility that the establishment communities are coalitions of distinct intra-party groups. We find some evidence of both, with variations by party. Establishment communities in both parties are inclusive of members from distinct factional caucuses, supporting the idea that presidential endorsement politics are an arena where many would-be factional actors set aside their differences to cooperate.

We conclude in Section 7 by assessing what our analysis tells us about party politics. It is common to speak of party factions, but they are sometimes treated as if they are to parties as parties are to the polity. This is not accurate. Factions are motivated to reshape the direction of their party, but they also want to cooperate with existing coalition partners. Hence our view that most are cooperating factions.

2 Party Factions

To most political scientists, political parties – particularly U.S. parties[1] – are *coalitions*. That is, parties are not groups of perfectly like-minded politicians, but rather teams bringing together differing interests. Partisans have differences, but they are willing to set them aside for collective gain. This need to build a stable coalition is central to why parties form in the first place.

Treating parties as coalitions is a flexible approach. For example, this approach allows us to think about parties as coalitions of completely distinct legislators, hoping to maximize their policy victories (e.g. Schwartz 1989) and to avoid instability (e.g. Aldrich 1995). Parties can stem from preexisting interest groups teaming up to win elections (e.g. Karol 2009; Bawn et al. 2012). They may be built around ideological cores or movements (e.g. Noel 2013; Schlozman 2016), and so on. Parties are likely all these things.

Scholarship on American parties has lately turned an eye toward the dynamics among different elements within the parties. Scholars have focused on an intermediate level of organization – the faction. A faction is a sub-coalition within a party that seeks to influence or reshape its party.

This academic interest echoes the attention that American party factions are receiving from journalists and other political observers. Factions are not new, of course, but the prevailing view of the contemporary major parties is that they are particularly rent by factions, struggling to hold themselves together. The Democratic Party is divided between "Progressives" and "Moderates" or "the Establishment,"[2] while the Republican Party has seen a takeover, in which a Tea Party turned "Make America Great Again" faction (Blum 2020), committed to Donald Trump, has effectively ousted the long-standing "Establishment," which reflected a different vision of conservatism (Hopkins and Noel 2022).

In this section, we outline the implications of factional divisions on the selection of the parties' presidential candidates.

---

[1] As we see it, this is true of parties everywhere, but in the United States' two-party system, where each party must bring together roughly half of the nation's politics, the coalitions are especially broad, hence our focus on U.S. parties.

[2] The scare-quotes here make clear that finding labels for these factions is fraught, a point to which we will return.

2.1 Theories of Faction

For many students of American politics, the idea of "factions" calls to mind James Madison's discussion, in *Federalist 10*, of "curing the mischiefs of faction." What Madison meant is slightly less precise than what we mean by the word, but his analysis is relevant. Madison was concerned that a group of citizens might want things that are at odds with the public interest and that they might capture control of the government to implement them. For Madison, a faction is any coherent interest or group that wants anything for itself.[3]

Madison thought to thwart such groups by creating a large, diverse republic with separated powers. Narrow interests in such a system would not be able to organize and capture the entire government.

But Madison was perhaps too optimistic about both the desirability and the effectiveness of his solution. Under the extreme fragmentation that he prescribes, very little can be accomplished at all. When political actors saw this problem and tried to resolve it, they created political parties (Schattschneider 1942). Political actors who represent narrow interests (e.g., Madison's factions) or even personal ambitions will seek out others to coordinate with. Even without Madison's hurdles, politicians will struggle to build careers in politics or advance any policy or social goals if they try to do it alone. They are more successful when they build a coalition with others. They are more successful still when those coalitions are "long" (Schwartz 1989; Aldrich 1995), in duration or even just in scope.

So, politicians form parties, uniting with other politicians who have their own goals. Some of these politicians' goals may be compatible with one another, some in conflict, and others in between. As members of a party, these political actors agree to compromise where they can and to yield where they cannot. They do so because there is strength in numbers, and the party is a necessary vehicle to achieve this strength.

In multiparty democracies, a smaller party can win seats or become part of a coalition that controls government. In the U.S. system, a party must have a chance at a majority, a reality that makes it difficult for smaller political coalitions to gain political influence on their own. This is where factions come in. They are the main vehicle for smaller political alliances to gain influence in politics in the United States.

Analogous to the parties in a multiparty coalition government, the factions in U.S. parties have their own focuses, and they unite with other groups or factions

---

[3] Some readers treat "faction" as synonymous with "political party," but Madison was not thinking of anything as well organized as modern political parties.

to form a majority. They must do so before the election, rather than in parliament. U.S. parties are thus something like permanent pre-electoral coalitions. The internal factions are more fluid and less formal, perhaps, but serve a similar role.

2.1.1 Long Coalitions and Factions

To understand how factions interact with the larger party coalition, we look more closely at the Schwartz-Aldrich model of a legislature that leads its members to form a "long coalition." The long-coalitions framework is useful to us for two reasons. First, its logic precedes the development of any specific party institutions. Since any coordination on the presidential nomination takes place in the informal invisible primary, against a backdrop of weakened (Azari 2023) or hollowed out (Schlozman and Rosenfeld 2024) formal parties, we want a framework that explains the broad incentives independent of those institutions. Those institutions do matter, as we discuss throughout this section, but the incentives do not depend on them.

Second, this framework is explicitly oriented toward the incentives to form a coalition against the incentives to pursue goals alone. It captures exactly the tension we are interested in, even without the coalition-forcing role that Polsby argued the convention provides.

The basic logic can be illustrated with a simple legislature with three members, A, B, and C, considering a series of bills, starting with these three.

In Table 1, each bill gives one legislator (or their district) something and costs another legislator/district something. The third legislator is unaffected. We could set this up in different ways. The set up in Table 1 follows Bawn (1999), who highlights cases where some actors have a goal, others oppose that goal, and still others are indifferent. For example, some people want to

Table 1 Payoffs for legislators over different bills.

	Legislator or "Group"		
	A	**B**	**C**
Bill 1	gain	indifferent	loss
Bill 2	indifferent	loss	gain
Bill 3	loss	gain	indifferent
⋯		⋯	⋯

expand abortion rights, others want to limit abortion, and still others don't really care.[4]

With the preferences in Table 1 and a simple legislative setting with an agenda and majority rule, we can consider the strategies that the actors might take. In such a game, what happens with each bill depends a lot on what the indifferent actor does. For example, A might persuade B to vote for Bill 1 on its merits. Or A might pledge to oppose Bill 2 to gain the support of B on Bill 1. But A and B would have a harder time agreeing on Bill 3, prompting both to look to C for help. And C might demand their support on Bills 1 or 2 (or future bills that are like those first two).

As they consider future legislation, the actors in our example might make such one-off agreements and short-term logrolls, sometimes being on the winning side, sometimes on the losing side. However, any majority of legislators (in this case two) could improve their lot by committing to *always* work together. A and B would need to find a way to resolve their disagreement on bills like 3, but that would be worth it to always have others' support on bills like 1 and 2. This is what Schwartz and Aldrich called a long coalition.

This logic generalizes to a larger legislature, as Schwartz and Aldrich explain. If a majority commits to forming a long-standing coalition, they will be able to get more policy wins for themselves (and their constituents) than if they construct a new coalition for every bill. This, they argue, is why parties form and why politicians work to hold them together. Bawn et al. (2012) work through this same logic outside the legislature, where the individual actors are social "groups" who may join forces to form parties. Instead of the "gentleman from Vermont" and the "gentlelady from California" forming a party, they would refer to "labor unions" and "civil rights groups."

The long coalition is an "equilibrium" in this game, meaning none of the actors will regret having participated after the fact. But it is also potentially fragile. To ensure success, ambitious politicians create institutions to help hold their long coalition together. "A political party is therefore more than a coalition," as Aldrich (p. 284) puts it. "A major political party is an institutionalized coalition, one that has adopted rules, norms and procedures." In the context of a legislature, these rules, norms, and procedures include legislative organization, in the form of party leaders and whips. Or in Bawn et al.'s application, they include nomination procedures to ensure the right candidates stand for the party.

---

[4] Other arrangements of preferences can highlight other features of legislative conflict. Schwartz and Aldrich start with a model in which each legislator has a preferred project with concentrated benefits for themselves, or their district, and diffuse costs to the entire legislature. This models distributive politics, where again parties are the solution that emerges.

Schwartz and Aldrich argue that actors create party institutions in response to the incentives they outline. But different institutions may be more or less effective at serving those incentives. Some institutions may even encourage undesirable behavior. The current system of public presidential debates, for example, gives potential candidates a major platform, encouraging the emergence of candidates who appeal directly to voters, independent of party coordination. But even if the nomination process is ill-suited to the task, it is where the coalition is formed and enforced. The mix of the informal and opaque invisible primary and the decentralized formal primaries and caucuses is where coalition formation occurs.

The institutions that help forge the party coalition are important because many different coalitions, or equilibria, are possible (Bawn 1999). To begin with, A and B can be in a coalition, but it is just as likely for A and C or B and C to form a long coalition. Once the two have committed to work together, they will benefit from that deal, but if something shakes their agreement, another partnership could be tempting.

Beyond *whom* is in the coalition, how the coalition members work out their disagreements and the relative strength of the members can also change. Long coalitions can vary in the commitment they demand from their members. They can demonstrate varying degrees of hostility to those outside the coalition. They can vary in the value they give to different coalition members, such that some groups in the coalition might get more than others. Some coalitions form among natural allies who have few internal disagreements, while others consist of strange bedfellows. *All* these possibilities are equilibria, and all are better than going it alone.

For instance, Bawn describes a difference in what she calls the "commitment" expected by the coalition. Bawn distinguishes between two equilibria, one of which expects subscribers of a coalition "to help their allies when costs fall on outsiders and to avoid imposing costs on allies but does not demand that subscribers take any action when outsiders threaten to impose costs on the ally." Or one arrangement might require two coalition members to always split the difference evenly on issues where they disagree, while another would systematically favor one partner over the other. Any of these arrangements can be an equilibrium, but they are all different.

It makes sense that, even if long coalitions are desirable, different actors will have different preferences over which long coalition would form, and what kind of coalition it will be. Conflict over either of those questions can lead to factions. A faction, in other words, might want a wholly different coalition, ejecting some members and bringing in others. But it also just might want the same coalition to be less willing to compromise with the other party or to just shift the balance of power among coalition partners.

But intra-party conflict over the nature of the coalition is different than inter-party conflict. It is not a mirror of general politics, replicated at a smaller scale.

2.2 Factions as "Groups" versus Factions as Strategies

One way to think about who the factions are is to look at the groups that join to form a party. In the toy example, A and B could be factions in the long coalition that includes them both. Factional conflict might involve the trade-off on bills like 3, where A and B are opposed. Maybe they have decided to compromise on these issues. Maybe they have decided to mostly keep them off the agenda, just as the Northern and Southern Democrats, as factions in the party during the New Deal Coalition, tried to keep civil rights issues off the agenda.

Of course, most parties are made up of more than two distinct interests, as in our toy example. But a party with several groups might still be divided between one set of groups and another set. Some of these groups might even leave one party and join another, as pro-segregation Southern Democrats did in the mid twentieth century.

These groups-as-factions are interesting, but most factions are of a different arrangement. The social groups that Karol (2009) and Bawn et al. (2012) describe are rarely monolithic. They can have internal disagreements about substance and strategy. What happens when some religious conservatives, for example, are willing to compromise on abortion restrictions, but others are not?

To illustrate, we expand our simple three-person legislature to something larger. Here, consider the case where each group is internally divided.

In Table 2, we have broken groups A, B, and C each into two subgroups: A1 and A2, B1 and B2, and C1 and C2. The A's have the same general interests and goals, and likewise the B's and the C's, but they may differ on other things. For

Table 2 Payoffs over different bills, with groups fragmented.

	Legislator or "Group"					
	A1	**A2**	**B1**	**B2**	**C1**	**C2**
Bill 1	gain	gain	indifferent	indifferent	loss	loss
Bill 2	indifferent	indifferent	loss	loss	gain	gain
Bill 3	loss	loss	gain	gain	indifferent	indifferent
...	...	...	...	...	...	...

example, A1 might be labor activists who, while wanting a much higher minimum wage, think the best way to get that is through incremental progress, while A2 are labor activists who would not accept anything short of a particular national minimum wage. B1 might be criminal justice reformers who think slogans like "defund the police" are polarizing and think body-cameras and increased oversight have more appeal to the public, while B2 are those who find such half measures insufficient or even counterproductive. In other words, these are differences over strategy, not substance.

A1 and A2 might also just disagree about who are the best leaders. Individual candidates for office usually represent some kind of vision for the party, including over the questions we've just raised. But they also are just people, some of whom hold special appeal to particular people. The policy orientations of Barack Obama and Hillary Clinton did not differ much, for example, but their appeals did. Now we can illustrate intra-party organization alongside inter-party conflict. The A's and B's could all be in a coalition, but different members of each group have strong preferences about how the coalition should work, or who should lead it. One faction (A1 +B1) seeks to compromise with the other party when possible and to present a more moderate platform, in the hopes of winning more swing voters. The other faction (A2+B2) thinks the first faction has sold out their principles and wants to present a more ideologically pure platform and be less willing to compromise with the other party.

This kind of conflict – whether described as moderate versus ideological, insider versus outsider, or pragmatist versus purist – has characterized many factional divides in both parties in recent years. For example, the recent tension between the Progressive wing of the Democratic Party and its mainstream wing is not so much about which groups should be part of the party coalition, but about how the party should approach the goals of the existing coalition. Bernie Sanders' challenge to Hillary Clinton and later Joe Biden did not seek to change who makes up the Democratic Party. All three of these candidates would count labor unions, underrepresented racial groups, and working-class voters as part of the party. But Sanders wanted to shift the party's emphasis to class over race and other identity politics issues, saying:

> . . . this is where there is going to be a division within the Democratic Party. It is not good enough for somebody to say, 'I'm a woman, vote for me.' No, that's not good enough. What we need is a woman who has the guts to stand up to Wall Street, to the insurance companies, to the drug companies, to the fossil fuel industry. In other words, one of the struggles that you're going to be seeing in the Democratic Party is whether we go beyond identity politics. I think it's a step forward in America if you have an African-American CEO

> of some major corporation. But you know what, if that guy is going to be shipping jobs out of this country, and exploiting his workers, it doesn't mean a whole hell of a lot whether he's black or white or Latino. (Rios 2016, see also Arceneaux 2016)

That's like giving more to A and less to B, but crucially, it is not about giving nothing to B or pushing B out of the party. Sanders was not arguing that these identity issues are not important, or that the voters and activists who care about them are not part of or should not be part of the Democratic coalition. Rather, he argued that focusing on class first was the best approach (Dann 2015; Otterbein 2019). And one of the ways Sanders shifted his campaign between 2016 and 2020 was to make that latter part clearer.

Sanders and other progressives also claim that the party is too quick to compromise on policy fights to win over moderate voters and wealthy donors. Sometimes this takes the form of claiming that mainstream Democrats don't care about working-class voters, or about other groups that are in the party. But progressives don't claim that mainstream Democrats want to exclude those voters, only that they take their votes for granted. This is the crux of the idea that Democrats "abandoned" the working class – working-class voters are supposed to be part of the Democratic coalition, but they are not getting what they should. In our extension of the long-coalitions model, this is the difference between A1 and A2.

A similar dynamic is taking place on the other side of the aisle. The main cleavage in the Republican Party today is between MAGA supporters of Donald Trump and more traditional Republicans, such as George W. Bush, Mitt Romney, and Elizabeth Cheney. That MAGA wing is the successor to an earlier Tea Party insurgency against the mainstream of the party (Blum 2020). Since Trump's nomination in 2016, however, that insurgency has largely succeeded in capturing control of the party.

The Tea Party and especially the MAGA movement differ from other Republicans on the party's direction. Tea Party/MAGA Republicans care more about cultural issues, oppose immigration, support trade barriers, and are more isolationist, particularly with respect to Russia and Ukraine. Many other Republicans would prioritize economic issues, free trade, and a more robust American presence abroad.

But again, in terms of the long-coalitions model, there are many groups in both factions, corresponding to our treatment of A1 versus A2. Some differences are about how strict policy should be on, for example, immigration. Others are about priorities around which issues can be compromised on, and which cannot. Some are about willingness to work with Democrats. And a lot of the difference is simply between those who think Trump himself is good for the party or the country, and those who think Trump himself is a burden. By splitting the groups in the Aldrich model into parts, we show how intra-party conflict is often about more than policy.

This conflict, while taking place inside one party, is always in the context of the whole polity. It would be too simplistic to just focus on the first four columns of Table 2 and see what strategies those players should take to win at that stage. They are also aware of the next stage. A1 needs A2, and they both need B1 and B2. The institutions that hold together the coalition are meant to allow intra-party disagreement to be resolved without undermining the coalition in the next stage.

This approach to thinking about factions will help us frame three important threads in the literature on factions.

2.2.1 Factions Are Not Groups, but Coalitions of Groups

In the group-centered theory of Bawn et al. (2012), parties are made up of interest groups and activists who have policy goals. These "policy demanders" form alliances with other such groups that are large enough to compete for election. In Bawn et al.'s expository hypothetical, organized groups of "coffee growers" and "saloon keepers" ally with "teachers" to get policies that each group wants.

But factions are not like the individual groups in that illustration. They are coalitions within parties. As coalitions, factions are made up of multiple groups and appeal to multiple constituencies within the party.

Such a sub-coalition within the party *might* represent a different subset of groups. It also may advocate for a different arrangement among the groups.

Focusing on factions within the legislature, Ruth Bloch Rubin (2017) and Andrew J. Clarke (2020) describe the Republican Main Street Partnership, the House Freedom Caucus, and the Democratic Study Group as organized factions or blocs. If the Republican coalition includes religious conservatives and small-government business leaders, the House Freedom Caucus includes them both as well. In her deep dive into the Tea Party, Blum (2020) describes a faction of the Republican Party that is more ideologically extreme and less trusting of the party establishment. The Tea Party did not bring in "groups" that were completely foreign to the rest of the Republican Party, but it did empower fringe groups and reconfigure the power arrangements internal to the party.

The defining character of these factions, though, is not what they want, but how behave with respect to their host party.

2.2.2 Factions Seek to Reshape Parties

Factions differ from parties. This could translate into a shift in policy priorities, group influence, electoral strategy, and more. Again, the analogy to multiparty democracy is illustrative. Over time, the parties that make up governing and opposition coalitions shift in importance, from senior partner to junior partner to excluded.

This is the story of the two major parties' shifting coalitions since the Civil War. The Republican Party, founded to advance an anti-slavery agenda before the war, is now the party most likely to defend memorializing the confederacy. The Democratic Party's agrarian roots stretch back to Andrew Jackson or Thomas Jefferson, but today the party is strongest in cities.

These changes are in large part due to the efforts of party factions. As DiSalvo (2012) puts it, factions are "conveyor belts of ideas" into the parties, ushering in new ideological (Noel 2013) or strategic coalitions for the party. The broad party change of the middle of the twentieth century might be described as the Southern Democrats' decline of importance in the Democratic Party and their eventual reorganization as a part of the Republican Party. As this happens, interests within each party rise and fall in influence and can even change what they ask of parties (Karol 2009).

This is why it is both useful and limiting to think about intra-party conflict as an analog to inter-party conflict. On the one hand, the faction is to the party as a party is to the polity, because capturing control of the party is a key intermediate step. But it is only an intermediate step. The faction is also interested in shaping how the party competes at the next level of contests: those between the two parties.

2.2.3 Factions Compete over the Machinery of the Party

Under the long-coalitions framework, everyone is better off if everyone remains in the coalition. But there are incentives for individual actors or groups to break away. Political parties create institutions to help keep their members in line. This "machinery" is the party's main asset. It has control of a nomination. It has control of an agenda. But who in the party gets to exercise that control?

Factional conflict is about that question. In 1983, James Sundquist described the parties as "terrain" to be fought over by different groups. The winner of control of the party's reins gets to shape its policy agenda. This competition is central to our conception of a faction (see Blum in press). Factions are movements or alliances that turn their eye to the party institutions themselves.

This is one way in which factions are to intra-party politics as parties are to the broader politics of the country. Unlike minor parties in a multiparty democracy, factions do not primarily compete independently for support from the public and then bring that support to the coalition. To be sure, voters can be aware of factions, and those factions may be useful "sub-brands" within the party (e.g. Clarke 2020), but the factional strategy is one of pressuring the party.

Following Blum (2020), we think this strategy can take two general forms: bridging or dividing. In both cases, as intra-party coalitions, factions seek to achieve influence by controlling the internal levers of party power. Long-standing factions might oscillate between these forms based on how friendly or hostile the party is to their efforts, and how strong or weak the party is electorally.

Some factions take a more cooperative approach. Members of these factions think the best way to increase their influence over the party's machinery is to provide a *bridge* between an important or new electoral constituency and the party. The Christian Right of the 1980s is one such example (see also Cohen 2019). They achieved influence by weaving their policy priorities into the goals of the Republican Party, recruiting like-minded candidates to run for office, and providing the Republican Party with a new voter base of evangelical Christians. The Republican Party, in turn, welcomed the Christian Right and its policy goals into their coalition. Although members of the Christian Right were not necessarily passionate about the goals of the other members of the Reagan coalition (primarily, economic libertarians and defense hawks), they were not opposed to these goals either. It cost the faction little to support these goals, and they received support for their goals in turn.

Other factions take a more insurgent approach. Members of these factions seek to create divisions *within* their host party as a means of heightening their own influence. Insurgent-style factions are willing to undermine their party publicly and in head-to-head contests. As an early example, take the New Right faction that supported Barry Goldwater's 1964 Republican presidential nomination. At the time, the conservative wing of the Republican Party had little influence or credibility within the party. They increased their influence through a concentrated effort to wrest control of the presidential nominating process from the party establishment.

The Tea Party is a more recent example. Rather than focusing on the presidency, this faction sought to remake the party by forming a shadow party apparatus that fielded Tea Party candidates against establishment Republicans in local, state, and congressional primaries. After enough Tea Party victories, the faction came to control many state and local Republican Party organizations, which allowed it further control over the party's machinery. Some factions take a hybrid approach – selectively opposing their party's nominee in certain contexts, while cooperating in others.

The Southern Democrats of the mid twentieth century, for instance, were much more conservative than the rest of their party and occasionally supported their own candidates in Democratic nominating contests. They were also willing to compromise with the rest of their party on labor issues in exchange for holding the line on segregation. The progressives of the twenty-first century similarly support their own candidates in certain nominating contests. They are nevertheless willing to compromise with the rest of the party by supporting establishment candidates and legislation that falls short of their policy goals in exchange for a say over the party's rules.

Those who take the cooperative approach are often described as "establishment," precisely because they prioritize winning and compromise over ideological purity. But insurgents can take control of the party and effectively become a new establishment. Eric Cantor, Kevin McCarthy, and Paul Ryan wrote the book on a *Young Guns* (2010) strategy to take over the party from the staid Republican establishment. They then moved into leadership themselves, only to be targeted by the Tea Party and MAGA movements a generation later. We will mostly use the word "establishment" to describe those who currently dominate and broker coordination within the party, even if they once had an insurgent past.

Whatever form their strategy takes, factions want the same thing as the rest of the party: electoral victory. Intra-party conflict is about members of the party coalition differing on the extent to which they support compromise, at what stage of the electoral process, and through which means.

2.3 The Distinctive Nature of U.S. Factions

Our characterization of factions focuses on the United States. Of course, parties in multiparty systems also can be internally divided. But the United States is an outlier in two important respects – the robustness of its two-party system and the openness of its candidate nomination process.

Several institutional forces combine to make the U.S. among the most aggressively two-party systems in the world. Other democracies with single-member districts and plurality rule tend toward fewer parties, but most still have influential if small third parties (Dunleavy 2012). But the United States has other features that are thought to restrict the number of parties – including its strong presidentialism and its Electoral College. Regardless of the reasons that the U.S. is an outlier, it is. The U.S. system discourages third parties.

In addition, the internal workings of U.S. parties are unusually democratic. No other democracy uses primaries to the extent that the United States does, and there are almost no formal party barriers to seeking nomination to the office of president. Indeed, this may be another force limiting the demand for third parties: Those who feel unrepresented by the current party coalition have a path to pressure for change from within, and thus have fewer incentives to form another party outside the existing ones.

These two factors help explain why divisions that might form the basis of different parties in other democracies become factions in the United States. While it is sometimes tempting to describe internal divisions within the major parties as the "true" or "natural" parties of our politics, it matters how the party system organizes and unites groupings of like-minded politicians into actual parties. As Clark and Golder (2006) find, democracies get many parties when two conditions are met: first, multiple cleavages provide the incentive to create multiple parties and then second, the electoral system allows them to be expressed. In the United States, institutions mask those divisions.

That masking matters. In a multiparty system, the groupings we describe as A1+A2 can form a small party and win. They do not need to think about the intermediate step of controlling a party. They just create their own. In most democracies, coalitional change occurs with the birth of new parties and the death of old ones (e.g. Bartolini and Mair 1990; Emanuele and Chiaramonte 2019). Many major parties in multiparty democracies began as factions within existing parties (Rosenbluth and Shapiro 2018). In contrast, the United States has had the same two major parties for over a century, and change occurs when internal factions grow, shift, enter, or leave the major parties.

Of course, intra-party factions can still occur in multiparty systems. But those factions are much more fluid and can even form their own parties. For example, the more centrist faction of the Italian Partito Democratico (PD), sometimes called the Renziani after leader Matteo Renzi, sparred with its leftist wing. While both sides sought control of the party, some leftists chose to leave, including running an alternative list under as Liberi e Uguali (Free and Equal) in the 2018 parliamentary elections. In 2019 Renzi himself left the PD to form a new party, Italia Viva (Italy Alive), bringing along a few dozen PD members. In the Italian example, control of the party was a prize to be fought over, but there were other strategically sensible options.

Since those options do not exist in the United States, intra-party conflict is much more important for the evolution of governing coalitions. And the choice of the presidential candidate is central to that conflict.

2.4 Factions in Nomination Politics

If controlling the machinery of the coalition is what a faction wants, nominations are a prize for them to compete over. And the presidential nomination is the ultimate such prize. It is thus not surprising that the factional politics we are describing play out in presidential nominations. It is easiest to describe the cleavage in the Democratic Party as between Sanders and a more moderate candidate like Hillary Clinton or Joe Biden. And it's even more natural to talk about the Trumpers versus the anti-Trumpers in the Republican Party.

In that context, members of a faction have an incentive to fight hard to ensure that the nominee is acceptable to them – and ideally one of their own. At the same time, however, party members and candidates want to bridge existing divisions. From the point of view of the members of the party who are not running for office, the party wants a candidate who can unite factions for two reasons. First, a unifier is more likely to win in the general election. And second, once elected, a unifier will be better able to govern.

Candidates themselves have a third reason to want to bridge factions, which is that they want to win the nomination itself. One *can* thread a path to the nomination by playing up one's factional appeal. This was the crux of Nelson Polsby's (1983) criticism of the post-reform system. A candidate with narrow but intense support, as from a specific faction, can come in first in early contests, parlaying that success into more money, more attention, and more excitement in later contests. In 2016, Donald Trump succeeded with precisely this strategy. He led with pluralities in early polls and leveraged that into a victory in part because the rest of the party did not coordinate around any one opponent (it is possible that Trump might have secured a majority against a single opponent, but he didn't have to). The Republican Party was already fractured over the Tea Party, which made room for Trump to succeed, even before he became a clear successor to the Tea Party movement (Noel 2016b; Blum 2020).

But as Cohen et al. (2008, 2016) argue, others in the party don't want to see this kind of narrowly factional strategy succeed, and if they unite around a consensus candidate, they can often stop it. Thus, a candidate may consciously try to appeal to multiple factions. This is more common. For example, in 2020, eventual nominee Joe Biden was positioned as a more moderate option, but he made several high-profile commitments to more progressive causes, like appointing a black woman to the Supreme Court or providing for student loan forgiveness (Biden 2020). In 2024, when the factional conflict within the Republican Party resolved around Trump and his MAGA movements, Nikki Haley rarely criticized Trump on substance: "I agree with a lot of his policies, but the truth is, rightly or wrongly, chaos follows him" (Kinnard 2023).

With both strategies in play, the resulting field of candidates will include those who appeal mostly to one or another faction, but also some who appeal – with differing degrees of success – to multiple factions. Any one endorser representing a faction might have several reasonable options. And any two endorsers from that same faction might make different choices among those options. The desire to find a candidate who bridges factions might be especially strong within the mainstream, establishment faction, given that this faction is more interested in compromise in the first place. But in a healthy party, even ideological factions may still be attracted to a more mainstream candidate who reaches out to them.

Such behavior would make party factions hard to detect. Not only will different people with similar preferences have different views about how the coalition should be structured (be in different factions), but they will also have different views about which person will do the best job managing those factions (and so endorse different candidates). Any two people within the same faction, or even any two people from within the mainstream part of the party, may make different choices in their support for the president.

All this conflict and cooperation takes place within the party's institutions. And those institutions will shape what can be done, and what we can observe.

For instance, the institutions that the U.S. House of Representatives uses to select its speaker are different from the institutions used to nominate a president. The Republican Party's struggles to select a Speaker of the House in 2023 illustrate one way that factions could manifest. After the 2022 midterm elections, Republicans held a narrow 222 to 213 majority in the House, a margin of only 4 votes. The Republican caucus' choice for the speakership was Kevin McCarthy, but a dissatisfied faction of Republicans broke with their party, and the chamber voted 15 times before McCarthy was able to secure the required 218 votes. Ten months later, that narrow majority crumbled again when eight Republicans voted to remove their party's leader from office.

Both of those conflicts were characterized, accurately we think, as a factional clash between the mainstream of the party and a right-wing, ideologically uncompromising faction.

The conflict over McCarthy reflected a broader factional conflict. Since the 2010s, s Tea Party/MAGA faction, represented early on through the Tea Party and Liberty caucuses and later through the House Freedom Caucus, has not shied away from open intra-party conflict (Blum 2020). Some members of this faction thought McCarthy was too compromising, and some reacted differently. For example, Jim Jordan, a House Freedom Caucus member, and frequent critic of the mainstream in the party, was put forward as an alternative candidate to McCarthy in January, and then again ran in October. But Jordan himself supported McCarthy in January. We don't think it is accurate to exclude Jordan, or other McCarthy supporters like Marjorie Taylor Greene, from this faction. They simply approached this specific conflict differently, possibly for personal reasons.

The institution used to select presidential nominations is different – and far less easy to control. Nominees are chosen in primaries, but politicians have ways to influence the process. Cohen et al. (2008) argue that party leaders get involved by expressing their support for their candidate and that this support can be influential. If the system that the House of Representatives uses is vulnerable to factional breakdown, the informal process might be more so. Even when they succeed, the result might be suboptimal. The Democrats' 2020 nomination of Biden, for instance, can be seen as a victory of unity over faction. But many in the party felt they were settling for Biden, an older white man amidst an otherwise exceptionally diverse field. Some other institution, like the conventions of the past, might have been able to elevate Kamala Harris, Cory Booker, Amy Klobuchar, or Pete Buttigieg, all candidates with similar appeal, but all also representing parts of the party that Biden did not.

In other words, in struggling to manage unity in the face of faction, the party muddles along. It is that muddling that generates our data.

As we explore in the next section, a network analysis of fifty years of endorsement decisions is a natural place to look for factional patterns in presidential nominations. Our design allows us to look across multiple decisions. This is necessary, as factional behavior will only emerge over repeated choices. Network methods also provide the tools to detect distinct communities of endorsers across these repeated choices, and to examine the possibility that these communities map onto factions.

But what we expect to find is the result of these conflicting incentives. In the terms of Cohen et al. (2016), we will find evidence of the incentive to unity and the incentive to faction, but we may not always identify the exact factions or establishment.

Instead, we expect to find communities that reflect the cooperating, coalition-managing behavior of the establishment, and other communities that reflect factions going their own way. Members of a faction might end up in either community, but the presence of both kinds of communities will show that both incentives are present.

3 Endorser Networks

The choice of a presidential nominee is perhaps the most central arena for intra-party conflict, making it a natural place to look for evidence of factions. Presidential nominations are not only a place where intra-party conflict plays out, but they are also a place where party members tend to cooperate (e.g., Cohen et al. 2008). Uncovering evidence of factional dynamics requires a specific type of data and a specific analytical approach.

Although voters in primaries and caucuses are responsible for selecting the nominee, voters are not the best place to look for factions. Instead, we look to the same data that Cohen et al. used to assess party influence – the record of party elites' endorsements of candidates for their party's presidential nomination. We should note that many political scientists call these endorsers "elites," and so will we, but that term connotes a level of exclusion that is not accurate. The arena of politically relevant actors in the party includes anyone with enough clout to get the attention of journalists.

Cohen et al. use these data to argue that party leaders effectively select the nominee, despite the openings in the system for outsiders to win the nomination on their own. Since Jimmy Carter surprised the party in 1976 (and through the book's release in 2008), no presidential candidate had won the nomination against the wishes of party leaders.

Party leaders are neither monolithic nor omnipotent, of course. Even before 2008, they were more united in some years than in others, notably 1988 and 2004 among Democrats. Internal divisions have seemed more common in recent years, including 2008 for the Democrats and 2016 for the Republicans. This is the result of what Cohen et al. (2016) describe as a tug-of-war between the incentive to faction and the incentive to unity. That tug-of-war is traced out in the patterns of endorsements we investigate here.

Of course, many other things besides elite endorsements affect who is eventually nominated (e.g. Norrander 1993; Mayer 1996; Dominguez and Bernstein 2003; Adkins and Dowdle 2005; Steger 2007; Dowdle, Adkins, and Steger 2009; Searles and Rose 2019; Bernstein 2019; Bernstein 2023; Conroy and Hammond 2023). But we are here less interested in the endorsers' success than in who they ally with when they back a candidate. It is enough that they think their endorsements are meaningful.

Endorsers no doubt have many motivations in deciding who to support and when, where, or even whether to announce their support. In addition to trying to influence the outcome, some may want to get on the winning side, back a friend, or something else. Some may decide not to support anyone publicly, even if they could be influential, to avoid opposing an ally. Even if all those other motives do not cancel each other out, we think we should still see systematic evidence of attempts to coordinate or attempts to back a factional choice.

3.1 Presidential Endorsements Data

Our data consist of every public endorsement for a presidential candidate in one of the two major parties' nomination contests between 1972 and 2020. We include any endorsement found in newspapers and magazines in the year prior to the primaries, up until the day before the Iowa Caucuses. Most of the data were originally collected for analysis by Cohen et al. The authors collected data from the 2008 through 2020 nominations separately, following the same procedures.

The Cohen et al. data collection procedure casts a wide net. One approach, common in the literature (e.g. Steger 2007) and in the media (e.g. FiveThirtyEight 2020, 2023), is to identify a set of relevant political actors, including perhaps members of Congress, governors, and state legislators, and then to search on each actor to identify whether they endorsed. This has the advantage of representing a well-defined population, but it can miss the permeable and informal nature of modern American political parties.

Instead, we include any endorsement that a journalist found notable enough to write up and publish. This approach captures influential party members who are not currently elected to a particular position, including former elected officials and high-profile politicos. Our approach also captures endorsements from individuals of more dubious importance, such as athletes and entertainers. We collected biographical information for all these endorsers, including (when applicable) birth year, gender, home state, and offices held (both at the time of endorsement and prior to the endorsement).

Cohen et al. developed a weighting scheme based on the perceived value of the endorsement and the endorser's importance to the party. We will make use of that same weighting procedure as explained in Table 3. We also have another filter to remove low-importance endorsers. For most of our analysis, we will use

Table 3 Endorser Weighting Index, adapted from The Party Decides (2008). Exception: Endorsers from Iowa, New Hampshire, a large state, or a major media market may receive a weighting boost of up to 0.1.

Tier	Weight	Endorser examples
1	1	Current president
2	0.9	Major national organizations like the AFL-CIO
3	0.8	Current Governor, other national unions, well-known or influential politicians (e.g., Hillary Clinton, Ted Kennedy)
4	0.7	Former president, major national organization with ties to the party (e.g., Christian Coalition, NOW)
5	0.6	U.S. Senator, leadership position in Democratic National Committee (DNC) or Republican National Committee (RNC)

Table 3 (cont.)

Tier	Weight	Endorser examples
6	0.5	Influential individual who's not a politician (e.g., Charleton Heston), influential member of the U.S. House (e.g., Speaker)
7	0.4	Former candidate for president, leadership position in the state legislature, U.S. House member, Mayor from a large city (e.g., New York City), well-known fundraiser, well-known celebrity with ties to politics (e.g., Barbara Streisand)
8	0.3	Former Governor, mayor of medium-large cities (e.g., Denver), former U.S. Senator, member of DNC or RNC, state office holder (e.g., Treasurer, Attorney General, Secretary of State); current executive cabinet member or executive appointee
8	0.2	Mayor of a medium city, member of the state legislature (not leadership), political consultant/lobbyist, local or state party official, former cabinet member or executive appointee, former aide to a prominent politician, former U.S. House member, president of a national organization
9	0.1	Municipal official (e.g., county supervisor, city councilperson, alderman, etc.), local branch of a national organization (e.g., union chapter), former candidate for Governor, celebrity with little history in politics (Shaquille O'Neal), newspaper
10	0	Intellectuals or practitioners (e.g., policy experts, attorneys, academics, or journalists) who are not well known, community organizer/activist who is not well known, members of state/local party chapter

only those who endorse more than once. To get into our data, an endorser needs to be viewed by at least one journalist as important in two separate nomination cycles.

The original data collection in Cohen et al. stopped at Iowa to ensure that a politician's decision to endorse is not being shaped by any electoral outcomes. Politicians could of course be influenced by polls, money raised, or media coverage of the candidates. However, Cohen et al. (see especially chapters 8 and 9) show that endorsements before Iowa seem to be largely independent of those other factors. It is still likely that endorsers are affected by considerations of "electability," but it is their own estimates of electability, not those revealed by electoral contests.

We are also concerned that the network of endorsers might be driven by the desire to get on the winners' band wagoning. If we want to uncover internal divisions, we need to observe behavior before too many elites switch to general election mode. But this does cost us some information. If key actors hold back until the candidates have proven themselves in a few state contests, we will miss their participation. In 2008, Barack Obama secured the support of several high-profile party insiders, including John Kerry and Ted Kennedy, but only after he received the plurality of votes in the Iowa Caucuses. Kerry and Kennedy were not band wagoning a candidate who was already assured of a win, although they were apparently reacting to an increase in Obama's probability of victory. Similarly, in 2020, Joe Biden received an influx of support, including from former fellow candidates, after his victory in South Carolina. Our approach to avoiding the influence of later events means we do not capture these kinds of dynamics.

And of course, our pre-Iowa endorsement data may still be susceptible to band wagoning. Cohen et al. demonstrate that endorsements do not appear to be driven by polls or other external factors, but there is no way to be sure that endorsers don't just have a better sense of who the eventual winner might be, independent of those variables. The existence (or not) of band wagoning doesn't matter for our argument. If factional actors overcome their differences just to be on the winning team, they are still not behaving in a factional manner. But they could be doing so for reasons other than the incentives we outlined in the previous section. We think there is enough evidence that band wagoning is not the only or even primary motivation, but it is probably still significant.

In addition to party leaders who are not in the data because they endorsed after Iowa, there are also many who do not endorse at all in one or another cycle. Since we are focused on patterns that play out over two or more cycles, that may mean that some high-profile figures are not included in our multi-cycle data.

In the end, the data we use here consist of every pre-Iowa link between an endorser and an endorsee from 1972 to 2020. Because most elites endorse only one candidate per cycle, the main links between endorsers come from their participation in multiple cycles. Thus, the network traces out long-standing patterns of support, rather than election-specific ones.

3.2 Social Network Analysis

Network methods are useful in studying political phenomena because politics often involves relationships (Lazer 2011). Some of these, including those we study here, are particularly complex constellations of relationships. These types of relationships are well-suited to SNA applications.

Network applications are diverse. Scholars have studied how networks form, how information or behavior flows through them, how the structure of the network affects other outcomes, and more. Our interest is similar to that of, for example, Yang et al. (2013), who looked at campaign donations in presidential nominations. In this section, we outline our specific application, and its implications.

Network methods treat the data as a collection of nodes (also called vertices) and edges (also called ties or connections). Nodes, in our case endorsers and candidates, are connected by edges, in our case the declaration of an endorsement.

Initially, this creates a *bipartite*, or two-mode network. That is, there are two kinds of nodes, endorsers, and endorsees. This structure is illustrated in the middle of Figure 1, which is based on a tiny part of our Democratic network.

This figure features four Democratic endorsers: Congresswoman Eddie Bernice Johnson (TX-30), Congressman Raul Grijalva (AZ-7), former mayor Bob Coble (Columbia, South Carolina), and Congresswoman Ayanna Pressley (MA-7). These endorsers all endorsed some combination of three candidates who ran in 2008, 2016, and 2020: John Edwards, Hillary Clinton, and Elizabeth Warren, as shown. Note that each candidate is listed with the year they ran. Endorsers can make new decisions in new contests. Someone who endorsed Clinton in 2008 and Clinton in 2016 would have arrows to each of those candidacies.

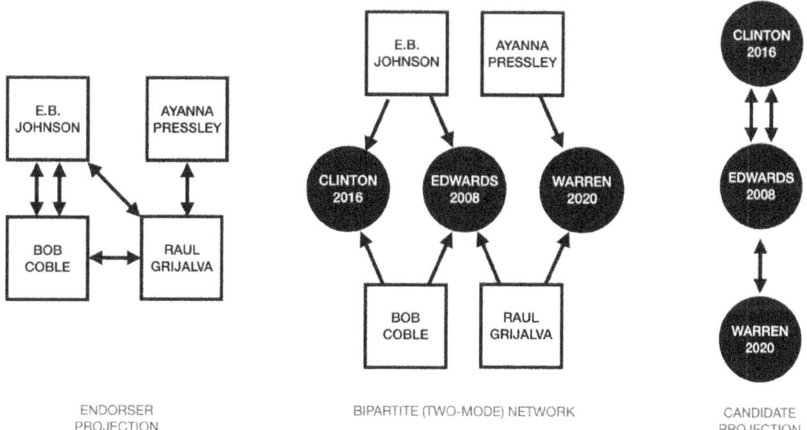

Figure 1 One-mode projections of two-mode networks.

Figures 2 and 3 present the bipartite networks, with both endorsers and candidates. Small circles represent endorsers. Larger squares represent candidates. Nodes are colored by the communities we detect in each part of the network, as we will discuss shortly.

Two-mode networks are usually transformed into one-mode networks before analysis, as most network measures are not well-defined for two-mode networks (Borgatti and Everett 1997; Latapy, Magnien, and Del Vecchio 2008). But our theoretical questions involve relationships among one kind of mode. We are interested in the connections among endorsers implied by their similar patterns of endorsement, or in the connections among candidates implied by their similar sets of endorsers.

For questions like these, two-mode networks can be projected into a one-mode network for either mode, as shown on the left and right of Figure 1. For purposes of illustration, we selected three candidates: John Edwards in 2008, Hillary Clinton in 2016, and Elizabeth Warren in 2020. These candidates have

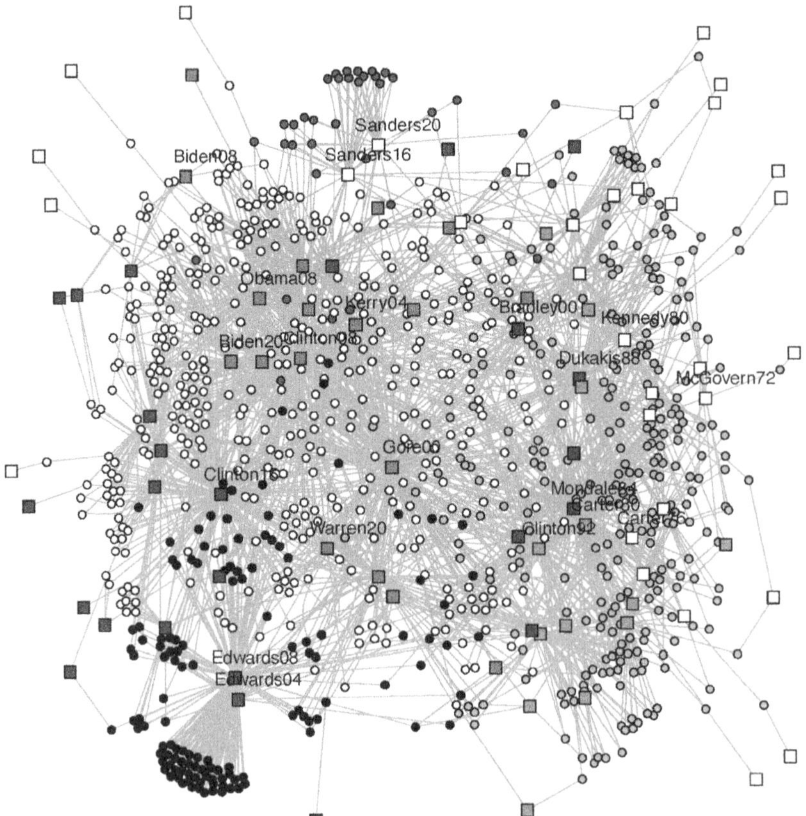

Figure 2 The Democratic bipartite network.

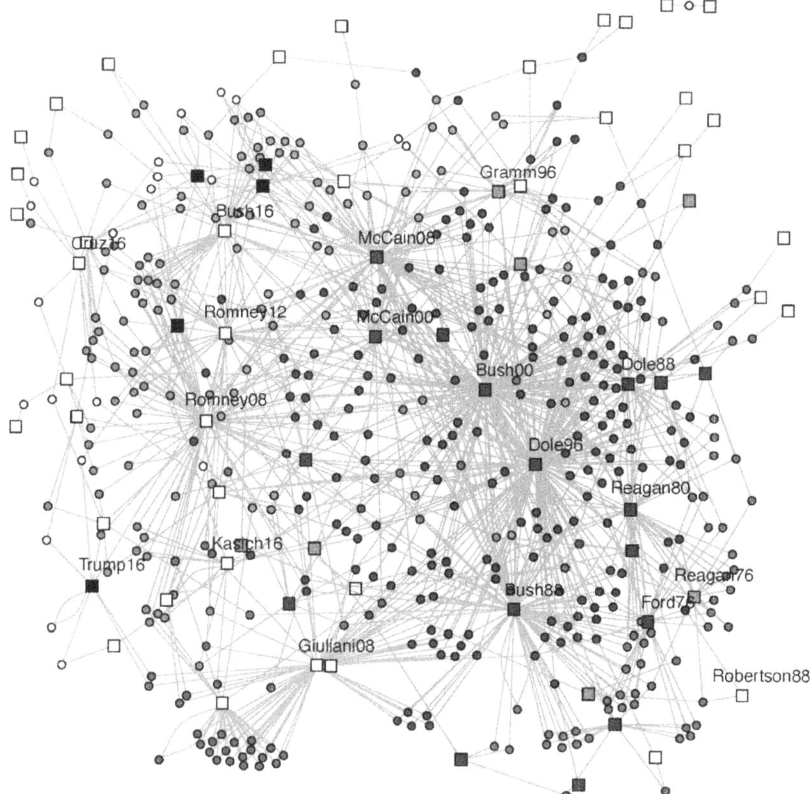

Figure 3 The Republican bipartite network.

distinct electoral profiles, and few endorsers supported all three. We show the pattern of four endorsers who endorsed at least one of these candidates.

On the left side, we have the endorser-by-endorser projection. There, we see that late U.S. House member Eddie Bernice Johnson (TX-30), an African-American woman whose political career began with Civil Rights activism in the 1960s, and (now former) Columbia, South Carolina mayor Bob Coble are linked by two shared endorsements. Both endorsed Clinton in 2016 and Edwards in 2008. They thus have two ties between them. U.S. House member Raul Grijalva (AZ-7) has only Edwards in common with Johnson and Coble, so there is one tie between Grijalva and each of them. Notably, both Grijalva and Johnson elected to back Obama instead of Clinton in 2008 after Edwards dropped out of the race, a tie not shown in this illustrative figure. In 2020, Coble, Grijalva, and Johnson's paths depart. Coble and Johnson backed Biden (not shown), while Grijalva supported the more progressive Elizabeth Warren (after backing Sanders in 2016). Grijalva's support for Warren in 2020 creates a tie with a different endorser, then-newly elected U.S. House member Ayanna Pressley (MA-7), who backed her home-state Senator Warren. Since Pressley only endorsed one of the three candidates – Warren in 2020 – she is only connected to Grijalva, who also endorsed Warren.

On the right, we have the endorsee-by-endorsee projection. Here, Clinton in 2016 and Edwards in 2008 have two connections, induced by Johnson's and Coble's endorsements of them both. Warren in 2020 has one connection to Edwards in 2008 based on Grijalva's endorsement of them both.

Before we create these projections, we drop all endorsers who only endorse one candidate because they do not represent long-standing participants in the party.[5] Including them would induce artificially large clusters around popular candidates but would not allow us to investigate the evolution of these clusters over time. The many endorsers who backed only Obama in 2008, for example, would all have ties to one another and not to anyone else.

Figures 4 and 5 show the one-mode endorser-by-endorser projection of both party networks. Again, the nodes are colored by the communities we detect in the next section.

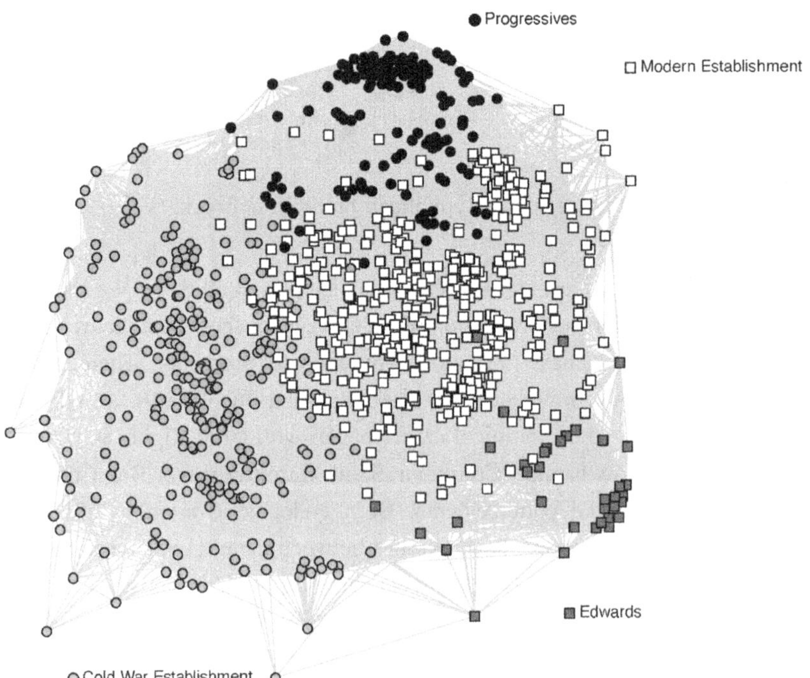

Figure 4 Democratic endorser-by-endorser network projection.

---

[5] This includes Ayanna Pressley, for whom 2020 was the first (and thus only) endorsement cycle. We show her endorsement in this figure for purposes of illustration.

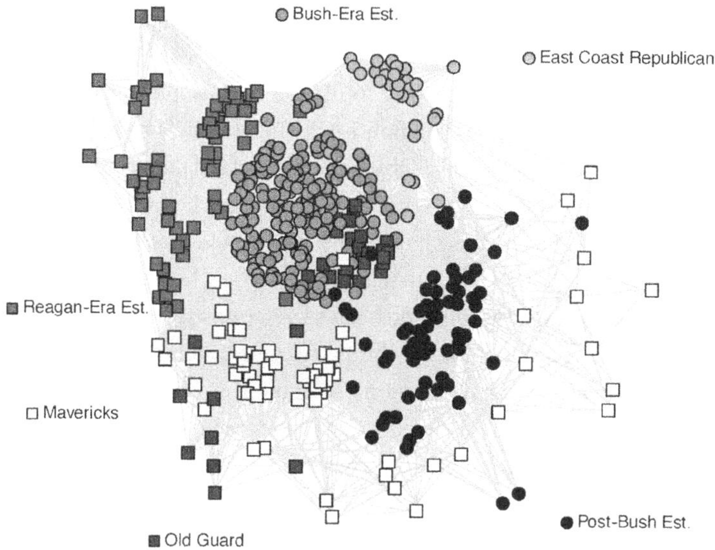

Figure 5 Republican endorser-by-endorser network projection.

3.3 Community Detection

These one-mode networks can be more readily analyzed to detect internal divisions. Methodologically, we treat these divisions as patterns of similarity in endorsement decisions. We detect these divisions using a clustering approach called community detection. Communities in a network are defined as a set of nodes that have many connections within the set and relatively few connections to other nodes.

We use the walk-trap algorithm to detect communities. The algorithm uses short random walks in the network to define communities, on the basis that such short walks are more likely to remain within communities than cross between communities. This makes short walks an efficient way of identifying communities. As Pons and Latapy (2005) show, the algorithm "surpasses previously proposed ones concerning the quality of the obtained community structures and that it stands among the best ones concerning the running time."[6]

Those with the same endorsement record will have a lot of ties between them and thus will be in the same "community." Those who have wildly different endorsement records will have few ties between them and will be in different communities. Allowing the algorithm to cluster endorsers based solely on

---

[6] The algorithm begins by computing a "distance" metric between every pair of nodes based on the probability that a short walk from one node reaches the others. The algorithm then clusters connected nodes with a low value of this metric. The resulting clusters are then iteratively joined with each other using the same approach. The algorithm identifies the division into clusters with the most intra-cluster ties and the fewest inter-cluster ties, and this is the division we use.

patterns in the data has the advantage of reducing the impact of researchers' biases on the results.

These communities give us a way to offer a more sophisticated answer to a common question in nomination politics: "who are the Bush people for?" or "who do the Clinton people like?" Observers understand that there are no "Bush people" exactly, but there are a set of people who backed the Bushes in their campaigns. We could simply ask how the people who endorsed George W. Bush in 2000 acted in 2008 and 2012, but identifying those who backed both Bushes, as well as whomever that group endorsed in 1996 (mostly Bob Dole) is a better way of identifying a subgroup of the party. Our community detection will identify clusters across all the patterns of support, even when someone sits out one race but otherwise follows the rest of the group.

The community detection algorithm finds four communities among the endorsers in the Democratic Party, labeled in shades of gray in Figures 2 and 4. The algorithm finds ten such communities among Republicans, only six of which are large enough to analyze in the coming sections. They are labeled in color in Figures 3 and 5. We also examine the candidate-by-candidate communities in Section 5. These are also labeled in Figures 2 and 3.

3.4 Communities and Factions

Are these communities we detect "factions," by the definition we laid out in Section 2? Not necessarily, for two reasons.

First, factions are partially defined by their strategy. They are a subset of the party that hopes to use the party's machinery to increase their influence in the party. By that definition, the establishment itself is not a faction and communities that reflect the establishment are not factions either. Communities that consistently act against the establishment, however, could very well be factions.

More importantly, party leaders' endorsement behavior may or may not be driven by factional concerns. Endorsers in a healthy party might be actively trying to find a candidate who can unite different factions. Those who are not interested in that kind of compromise might define a faction, but those who are interested will end up defining the compromise. This raises the possibility that many endorsers who represent party factions in other contexts might put aside these differences in the context of party nominations, joining in with the party establishment. In later sections, we explore the possibility that establishment communities might be coalitions of intra-party groups, including factions.

Finally, it is possible that the people who are not interested in compromise might eschew participation in the nomination process altogether, especially if they see it as rigged or illegitimate. This could result in the underrepresentation of certain factions with an anti-elitist ideology (e.g., the Tea Party) in the endorsement network.

We turn to interpreting these communities, and their relations to the concept of a faction, in the next section.

4 Establishment and Factions in the Parties

An adage, usually attributed to Bill Clinton, is that when it comes to presidential nominations "Democrats fall in love; Republicans fall in line" (e.g. Halperin and Heilemann 2013). This conjures an image of a fluid and passionate Democratic Party and a hierarchical and rational Republican one.

Clinton is not alone in identifying differences between the parties. The Republican Party is generally thought to prize symbolic ideological commitments, to disdain compromise, to be more internally hierarchical, and to draw from a more demographically uniform voter base for whom partisanship is an identity. At the same time, the Republican Party has been and continues to be more vulnerable to incursions from movement activists (Tarrow 2021), from Goldwater's New Right in the 1960s to the Tea Party of the 2010s. The result is a party characterized by a high degree of loyalty to symbolic conservatism (Ellis and Stimson 2012) and voters who are ideologically aware (Lelkes and Sniderman 2016) *as well as* internal disagreement about how to apply these ideals to specific policies (Hare and Poole 2014; Lupton, Myers, and Thornton 2017). This combination makes the Republican Party the site of rolling battles between factions.

The Democratic Party is often described as having a less rigid organizational structure and a less coherent ideological identity (Grossmann and Hopkins 2016). Beginning in the 1960s, the Democratic Party made a policy of including representatives from multiple groups and factions in its formal machinery and negotiations (Kamarck 2016; Blum in press). Perhaps because of this more flexible structure, perhaps because movements on the left tend to organize outside of the party system, the Democratic Party has suffered far fewer incursions from movements or factions, and it has typically resolved these episodes by deliberately incorporating factional members into the formal coalition. The Democratic Party's electoral coalition is also more demographically pluralistic, and its ideological commitments are more diffuse. Despite this, Democratic decision makers agree more consistently on specific policy priorities than do their Republican counterparts (Lupton, Myers, and Thornton 2017).

These broad characterizations of the two parties suggest, at least, that the presidential nomination politics may differ between the two major parties. At the same time, it should be clear that these observations do not always point in the same direction. And we are not the first to observe that the parties seem to have swapped when it comes to falling in line or in love (Mitchell 2011; Antle 2019; Klein 2023).

We thus begin looking at our party endorsement networks with the expectation that there may be significant differences between the parties. We don't necessarily bring strong priors about what those differences will be.

It may be that the parties are substantially the same. If they do differ, it may be that they are different in idiosyncratic or atheoretical ways, or there could be systematic differences in how rent they are by faction or how well the establishment seems to dominate.

4.1 Network and Community Measures

We systematically compare the parties in three ways.

First, we survey the networks, including how fragmented into apparent factions each is. Then we look at the divisions, or factions, within the network. Finally, we turn to the individual endorsers and their position within the network and within the identified divisions. Taken together, these levels of analysis paint a picture of the differences between the two parties' endorsement networks, and characterize the presence or absence of factional divisions within the parties.

An **overall picture of network activity** comes from the *number of endorsements* each party makes, the *number of endorsers* responsible for those endorsements (e.g., unique endorsers), the number of people who endorse more than once (e.g., repeat endorsers), and the number of people who only appear once in the data set (e.g., one-time endorsers). Our network-level analyses only consider repeat endorsers. These endorsers have a stake in the endorsement process over time, and endorsing more than once makes it possible to map connections between them in a network.

Understanding the relative coherence or divisions within the parties relies on other metrics. Network statistics that measure within-network unity (*density*) and within-network divisions (*modularity*) are a good starting place but are sensitive to factors like network size and the number of edges. In discussing internal network cohesion and division, we rely instead on a hierarchical clustering approach known as *community detection*. Community detection identifies distinct clusters of endorsements with similar endorsement behaviors. These groups might prove, upon further investigation, to be intra-party factions.

In our endorsement networks, a community is a subgroup of endorsers who tend to agree with one another on the nominee more often than they agree with other members in the network. The number and size of communities within both networks are informative but also limiting.

A network with fewer communities might be a more cohesive one, while a network with more communities might be less cohesive. Then again, a network with a few communities that are roughly the same size and defined by backing opposing candidates in the same contests would indicate a party rife with factional divisions. A network with the same number of communities where one community is very large and the others are relatively small would, conversely, represent a party with a cohesive core and some splinters of dissent.

Network divisions that develop over time are different than ones that divide the same period. The former would indicate cohort replacement, while the latter would speak to internal cohesion.

So, we turn to the **community-level characteristics**. These include *size*, as in the number of endorsers in each community, *internal cohesion*, or the density of connections within each community, and the *top candidates* who received the most cohesive support from within each community. We also consider *activity* and *timeline* by looking at the volume of endorsements from each community and when these endorsements are made.

We then look to **endorser-level characteristics** to see what types of actors are common in each community.

First, we consider the role of endorsers' *ideology* in defining communities (DiSalvo 2012). We can assign ideological scores to members of the network who served in Congress, ran for an elected office, or donated to a political candidate, using DW-NOMINATE and the Database on Ideology, Money in Politics (DIME). Many of our endorsers do not have any of these scores (itself informative), but there is enough to characterize the ideological divergence – or lack thereof.

Another common source of intra-party organization is region, so we consider the endorsers' *home states*. Representatives of certain states might act in concert, producing the appearance of a factional division where this isn't one. This might be especially true of states with larger delegations (e.g., California), early primaries (i.e., Iowa, New Hampshire, or South Carolina), and even the home states of certain nominees (i.e., Arizona for John McCain).[7]

We have other demographic variables on our endorsers, including *birth cohort* and *gender*. We code each endorser's birth year to examine the possibility of a cohort effect within communities.[8] All endorsers are coded as male or female based on available information.[9] We suspect that a community with

---

[7] All endorsers were coded for home state at the time of each endorsement. Endorsers tended to inhabit the same state throughout their endorsement careers, as most are politicians representing specific constituencies. If a state was not available, the endorser was coded as 'NA.'

[8] Organizations and newspapers, for example, are coded as 'NA' for birth year and for the next variable, gender.

[9] Available information did not identify any endorsers as non-binary, although we cannot rule out the possibility that such endorsers exist. The gender coding is meant to provide a broad overview of how overwhelmingly male the networks are or are not. Individuals with no identifiable gender information, along with organizations, are coded as "NA." We also did not code endorsers for another salient characteristic: race. Although this information is available for many higher-level

a higher-than-average number of women endorsers (women are the minority in the network) might differ systematically from communities with fewer women.

A final major area of consideration is each endorser's *role in the party*. Some network divisions could reflect the various roles in the party held by endorsers. For example, it is possible that organized labor has distinct interests within the Democratic coalition, or that state legislators will think about nomination politics differently than members of Congress. We bring together multiple measures of party role to develop a more accurate picture. These include the type of office held by endorsers (e.g., national, state, party, local, or none) and endorser weight. Using the weighting scheme from Cohen et al. (2008), we assign each endorser a weight in the network (ranging between 0 and 1) corresponding with their occupation or standing in the party to address the possibility that some communities are dominated by high-weight endorsers, while others are made up of low-weight endorsers.

Network *centrality* statistics provide another way to get at endorsers' roles in the party, and specifically at the relative connectedness of each community's endorsers to the party overall. We calculate these statistics at the level of individual endorsers and then compute averages within each community. We report two distinct but complementary measures of centrality: betweenness and closeness.

Betweenness captures the idea that the more people you connect with, the more central you are. Betweenness is based on the number of shortest paths between other network members that pass through each member. A community's average betweenness score tells us the extent to which the network is more connected if that community's endorsers are part of the network than if they are not (Patty and Penn 2016).[10]

Closeness centrality reflects the number of steps it takes to get from one actor to every other actor in the network. A community's average closeness score captures the relative connectedness of that community's endorsers. Taken together, these measures provide a snapshot of the importance of each community to the structure of the party endorsement networks.[11]

---

elected officials, coverage is spotty at best for lower-level elected officials and non-elected endorsers, especially in the earlier years of the data.

[10] This makes betweenness scores an important metric for research on other informal elite networks, such as policy and issue networks (Scholz et al. 2008; Skinner et al. 2012).

[11] Both measures have quirks based on the properties of the underlying data. Betweenness is sensitive to the distribution of connections in the network. A well-connected actor in a network made up of many connected actors would have a lower betweenness score than a well-connected actor in a network with fewer connected actors. Closeness assigns all actors an equal weight in the network rather than considering the varying levels of connections in the network, which can result in more ties. Considering these two scores together will provide a more comprehensive picture of power in the network than looking at either alone (Brandes et al. 2016). Betweenness

Taken together, the community- and endorser-level characteristics provide sufficient information to evaluate our hypotheses about the divisions within the networks. These features also help discern the extent to which any divisions map onto substantive factions and the extent to which they are idiosyncratic.

4.2 The Two Full Networks

Table 4 compares the Democratic and Republican endorser networks that we presented in the previous section on several dimensions. The first is the total number of endorsements made, or at least that journalists found worth reporting. Democrats have roughly 2,000 more endorsements than Republicans. The 6,728 Democratic endorsements were made by 5,366 unique individuals (around 1.25 endorsements per person), while the 4,660 endorsements in the Republican network were made by 4,057 unique individuals (around 1.15 endorsements per person).

For our purposes, the total number of endorsers or endorsements is less informative than the number of individuals who made repeated endorsements across presidential contests. Examining these individuals, the *repeat endorsers*, allows us to ascertain patterns in endorsements over time. Here, the two parties deviate even more. The Democrats have nearly twice the number of repeat endorsers as the Republicans (873 versus 422). The remaining endorsers in both networks only endorsed in one presidential contest.

The networks both have density statistics in the 0.2 range. This means that, for the Democrats, roughly 20 percent of all possible connections (i.e., shared endorsement behavior) are made. For the Republicans, that number is closer to

Table 4 Overview of Democratic and Republican endorsement networks.

	Democratic endorsers	Republican endorsers
Endorsements total	6,728	4,660
Unique endorsers	5,366	4,057
Repeat endorsers	873	422
One-time endorsers	4,493	3,613
Number of contests	11	8
Density	0.1996	0.255
Modularity	0.312	0.232
Communities	4	10

---

and closeness use different scales, and we report the scores using these original scales. These scales should not be compared directly to one another. Scores also cannot be compared across networks since the underlying data differ.

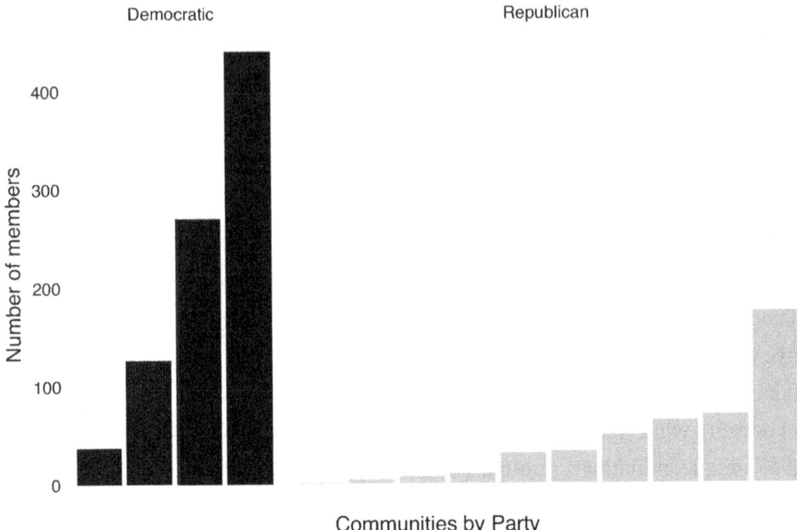

Figure 6 Communities in the Democratic and Republican Party
endorser networks.

25 percent. The Democratic network has a slightly higher modularity score than
the Republican network (0.312 versus 0.232). This signals the presence of
distinct groups of endorsers within both networks, with potentially clearer
divisions between groups in the Democratic network.

We can get a better sense of what modularity means from the number of
communities detected in each network. This is perhaps the area of greatest difference between the two parties. The Democratic network, though larger, has fewer
communities – four versus the Republicans' ten. Figure 6 plots the Democratic and
Republican communities side-by-side for comparison. Not only does the
Democratic Party have fewer communities, but they are larger than the communities on the Republican side. The smallest Democratic community has 37 endorsers
in it, and the largest is made up of 440 endorsers. For the Republicans, the smallest
community contains only one endorser who has an idiosyncratic pattern of
endorsements.[12] Three additional communities contain ten or fewer endorsers,
all following idiosyncratic patterns based on allegiance to specific candidates in
crowded election fields. Of the remaining six Republican communities, which are
the focus of our analyses, the smallest contains 31 endorsers, and the largest 175.

The Democratic Party seems, from this first glance at its endorsement
patterns, to both have more participation and fewer disagreements. The slightly
higher modularity score for the Democrats indicates that these communities

---

[12] This endorser was Kim Lehman, former Iowa RNC member.

may be more distinct from one another than the Republican communities are. That said, the Republican Party also shows less participation and consensus overall, with a smaller number of endorsers split up across ten communities. The amount of participation could also be an artifact of the different numbers of contested nomination cycles (e.g., in which party leaders made endorsements) between the two parties. There were eleven such cycles between 1972 and 2020 for the Democrats and only eight for the Republicans. That does not quite match the magnitude of the difference, but it is likely a contributing factor.

Identifying who these communities are requires us to look at the next levels of analysis.

4.3 Communities within Networks

4.3.1 Four Democratic Communities

The Democratic endorser network has four main divisions, or communities, based on endorsement patterns in presidential nominating contests from 1972 to 2020. We assign each community a descriptive name based on its key characteristics.

The two largest are consensus communities united around established candidates. On this basis, we call them "establishment" communities. The chief difference between the two establishment communities is time: One is characterized by endorsements in the Cold War Era, and the other by endorsements after the year 2000. So, we call them the "Cold War Establishment" and the "Modern Establishment."

The two smaller communities are more candidate-oriented. One is made up of supporters of John Edwards in the early 2000s, and the other of Bernie Sanders' supporters in the 2010s. The endorsers in these candidate-centered communities are more likely to occupy state-level political roles than national ones. They also deviate ideologically. Edwards' endorsers are more conservative than other Democrats, and Sanders' are more liberal. These communities reflect factions. We label them the "Edwards Backers" and the "Progressives."

As we uncover the community and endorser-level characteristics of the Democratic endorser network, we will find evidence of a party that tends to unify around consensus candidates. Key divisions relate to generational replacement (i.e., time). Although some party members depart from consensus in the 2000s to support specific candidates, these party members tend to be from the same state as the candidate in question, or newer to elected office.

Table 5 gives an overview of the communities in the Democratic network. It lists the descriptive name assigned to each community, the number of endorsers per community (size), the relatively internal unity of each community (density),

Table 5 Communities in the Democratic network.

Community name	Size	Density	Top candidates
Cold War Establishment	270	0.30	Mondale 1984, Dukakis 1988, Clinton 1992, Carter 1980
Modern Establishment	440	0.40	Clinton 2008 & 2016, Gore 2000
Edwards Backers	126	0.89	Edwards 2004 & 2008
Progressives	37	0.85	Sanders 2016 & 2020, Obama 2008

and the candidates endorsed by the highest proportion of community members, beginning with the most endorsed candidate/year.

The **Cold War Establishment** is the second largest, with 270 members, and the least cohesive than the first two. It has an internal density score of 0.30 out of 1, both due to the longer time frame over which its members were active and to the party's shifting identity in the 1980s. Despite the lower density score, the Cold War Establishment coalesced around candidates who became the party's nominees between 1980 and 1992. Walter Mondale in 1984 was the most popular, followed by Michael Dukakis in 1988, Bill Clinton in 1992, and Jimmy Carter in 1980.

The **Modern Establishment** is the largest with 440 members. It is more cohesive than the Cold War Establishment but less cohesive than the candidate-centered communities, with a density score of 0.40 out of 1. The Modern Establishment community united around the party's eventual nominees from 2000 to 2016. Its top choice was Hilary Clinton in 2008, then Clinton in 2016, followed by Al Gore in 2000.

The **Edwards Backers** community is the second smallest in the network, with 126 endorsers. It is also much more cohesive than the establishment communities, with a density score of 0.89 out of 1, likely because its endorsers all coalesced around John Edwards in 2004 and 2008. The **Progressives** community is the smallest, with thirty-seven members. Like the Edwards Backers, the Progressives are internally cohesive with a density score of 0.85 out of 1. Members of this community endorsed Bernie Sanders in 2016 and 2020. Those who participated in the 2008 contest supported Obama.

At least some of the divisions in the Democratic network are driven by time, as demonstrated in Figure 7. The two candidate-based communities are predominantly active in contests featuring their candidate of choice (2004 and 2008

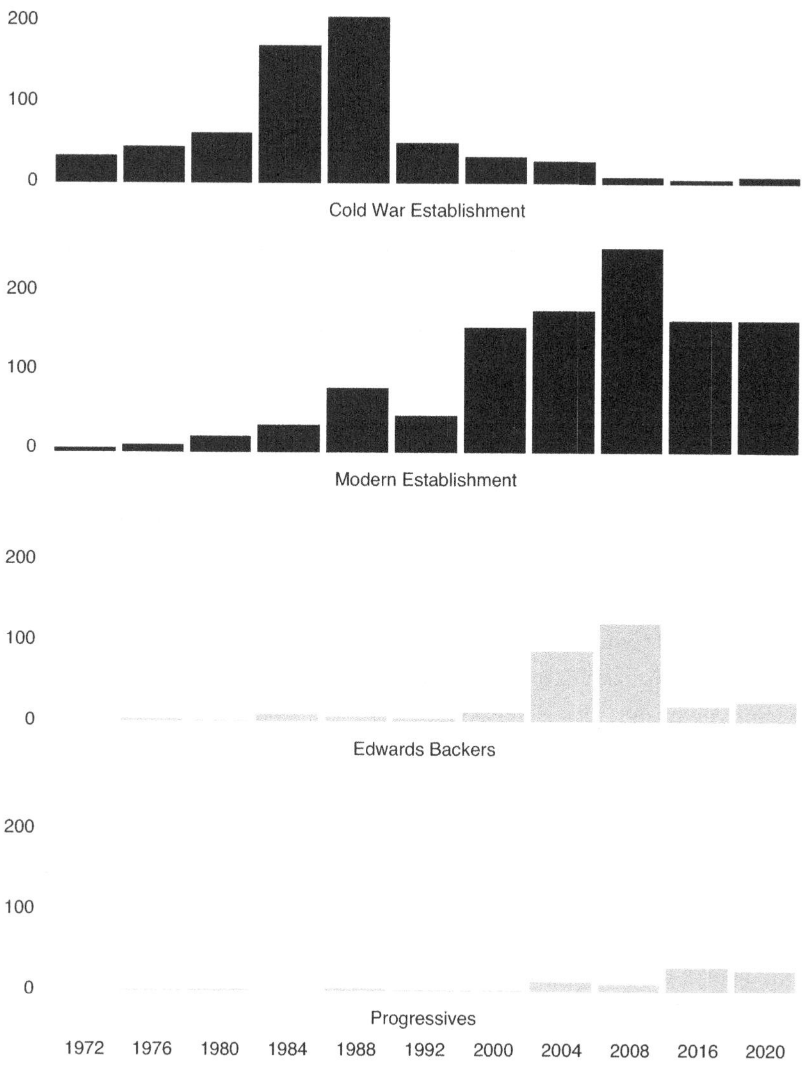

Figure 7 Endorsements of each Democratic community by election year.

for Edwards Backers, 2016 and 2020 for Progressives). The Cold War Establishment and Modern Establishment almost look like one community split across time. The Modern Establishment's endorsements pick up in 2000, where the Cold War Establishment's endorsements leave off. Right before that break, the 1996 cycle was not contested by Democrats, so the break happens exactly where we have less data to hold the groups together.

Notably, the two candidate-centered communities are contemporaneous with the Modern Establishment. This could mean that the party has experienced increased fracturing in the modern period. If we combine these time figures with the density information in Table 5, however, we recall that the Cold War Establishment is less internally cohesive than the modern communities. Unlike the modern party, the Democratic Party, of the 1970s and 1980s did not have any standout, non-establishment candidates like Edwards or Sanders to create clear splintering in endorsement patterns.

4.3.2 Six Republican Communities

We detect ten communities within the Republican network, but four are very small. These are a community of ten Huckabee supporters, one of seven Cruz supporters, one of four 2016 Trump supporters, and a disconnected outlier "community" that contains only one endorser.

Four of the remaining six communities can be characterized as the party establishment. Like the Democratic establishment, they include a succession of communities that are most active in a particular period in the party's history – the Reagan Era, the G.W. Bush Era, and the Post-Bush Era – and a group of very insider endorsers who bridge the Bush and Post-Bush Eras. We call this last group the "Old Guard."

The other two larger communities, like the very small ones, are focused on specific candidates. One is made up of endorsers from the New York and New Jersey area, backing local candidates Rudy Giuliani and Chris Christie. We call them "East Coast Republicans." The other repeatedly supported John McCain, so we call them "Mavericks."

Table 6 summarizes the ten communities in the Republican network.

With sixty-four members, the **Reagan-Era Establishment** is the third largest community. With a density score of 0.71, it is also the second most cohesive community. This community supported the contest winners in the 1970s and 1980s, with the greatest coordination around George H.W. Bush in 1998, followed by Ronald Reagan in 1980 and Gerald Ford in 1976.

The largest community is the **Bush-Era Establishment**, which has 175 members and is moderately cohesive with a density score of 0.56. This community unites behind the party's winners in 1996 and 2000, supporting Bob Dole and George W. Bush, respectively.

The **Post-Bush Establishment** community is the second largest in the network, with seventy members. It is also the least internally cohesive community, with a density score of 0.42 out of one. Members of this community coalesced around some of the most establishment-style candidates between 2008 and 2016, supporting Mitt Romney's candidacy in 2008, Jeb Bush's in 2016, and Romney's in 2012.

Table 6 Communities in the Republican network. Communities in italics are not included in the main analyses due to size.

Community name	Size	Density	Top candidates
Reagan-Era Establishment	64	0.71	Bush 1988, Reagan 1980, Ford 1976
Bush-Era Establishment	175	0.56	Dole 1996, Bush 2000
Post-Bush Establishment	70	0.42	Romney 2008, Bush 2016, Romney 2012
Old Guard	33	0.6	Romney 2008, Bush 2000, Dole 1996, Romney 2012
East Coast Republicans	31	0.95	Giuliani 2008, Christie 2016
Mavericks	49	0.45	McCain 2008, McCain 2000, Bush 2016
Huckabee Supporters	10	NA	Huckabee 2008, Fiorina 2016, Huntsman 2012
Cruz Supporters	7	NA	Cruz 2016
Early Trumpers	4	NA	Trump 2016
Outlier Community	1	NA	Brownback 2008, Santorum 2012

The final establishment community, the **Old Guard**, is also the smallest of the establishment groups, with thirty-three members. It is moderately cohesive with a density score of 0.6. Unlike with the other establishment communities, the Old Guard's endorsements are not confined to a particular period. Their activity overlaps with both the Bush-Era and Post-Bush Establishment, supporting Romney in 2008, Bush in 2000, Dole in 1996, and Romney in 2012.

We still treat the Old Guard as an establishment community, because of who they support.

This brings us to the candidate-centered communities. The **East Coast Republicans**, with thirty-one members, is the smallest community included in our main analyses. They are also the most cohesive with a density score of 0.95, demonstrated in their shared support of Giuliani in 2008 and Christie in 2016. The **Mavericks**, a community of forty-nine members with a moderate density score of 0.45, were most supportive of McCain in 2008, followed by McCain in 2000, then by Jeb Bush in 2016.

The remaining four communities, listed in italics in the Table, are too small to analyze in detail. They seem to be splinter communities made up of endorsers who support candidates with specific visions of the party that depart from the mainstream, including Mike Huckabee, Ted Cruz, and Donald Trump. Their existence is notable given the lack of such splinter communities in the Democratic network.

As with the Democratic communities, we see a pattern in time with our Republican communities, in Figure 8. There again is a succession of

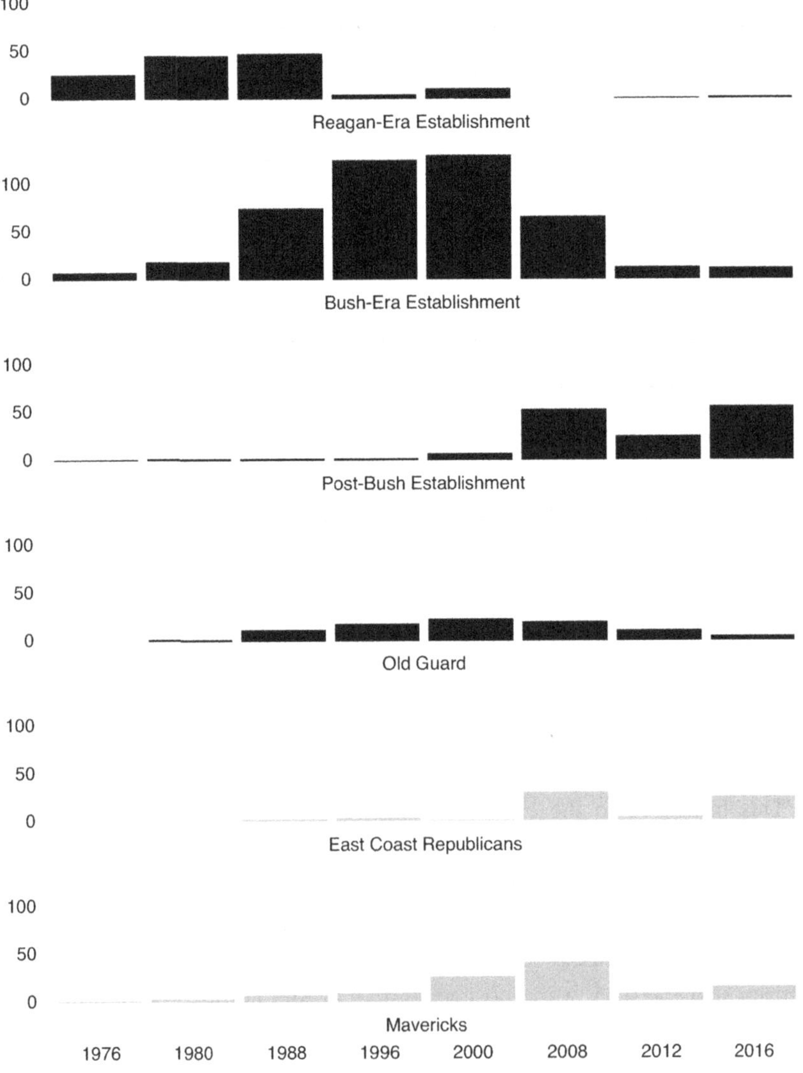

Figure 8 Endorsements of each Republican community by election year.

communities, as the Reagan-Era Establishment's endorsements taper off after the 1988 election, to be replaced by the Post-Bush Establishment, East Coast Republicans, and Mavericks, whose endorsements primarily occur after the year 2000. The Bush-Era Establishment and Old Guard bridge the gaps. Endorsements for the former build through the late 1980s to reach a peak in the contests immediately before and after George W. Bush's two terms (1996 and 2008), then taper off. Endorsements for the latter occur at a relatively steady rate from 1988 to 2012.

This broad overview suggests a Republican Party that has grown substantially less cohesive over time, but that had a strong establishment core for several decades before this trend began. That erosion coincides with the breakdown in the party's control of the nomination in 2016. As we noted in Section 2, Trump's nomination in 2016 was in part due to the party's inability to coordinate around a clear alternative. Why did they fail? These data suggest that, consistent with some existing explanations (Noel 2016b; Cohen et al. 2016), the Republican Party was increasingly divided along other lines when Trump entered the picture. While it is too early to see this in our data, we think we may have a novel way to trace the transformation of the party as it either coalesces around a new, MAGA-style vision of the party or reverts back to its pre-Trump coalition.

4.3.3 Establishment and Candidate-Centered Factions

In both parties, most of the endorsers are in what we are calling establishment communities, which support the eventual nominee. And in both parties, those communities have periodic breaks, as one generation yields to the next. The exact timing and number of the breaks between these establishment groups is probably mostly idiosyncratic, depending on when key endorsers begin and end their careers, and which nomination each party contests. The Reagan establishment was separated from the Bush establishment by two cycles, 1984 and 1992, in which Republicans were not active. Republicans were likewise not active in 2004. The break among Democrats occurs after the uncontested 1996 race.

Both parties also have had more fragmentation in recent years. All the smaller communities that we have labeled "candidate-centered" emerged in 2004 or later. According to our data, both parties were relatively cohesive in presidential nomination politics before then, and insurgent factions have been more significant since then. This does not necessarily mean there were no factions of note before. We know there were. But they did not manifest as clearly in nomination politics, where party consensus was much more common. This may reflect the irony of *The Party Decides*' publication date in 2008, right as the landscape it describes was changing (see Cohen et al. 2016).

Are these smaller communities really "candidate-centered"? The candidates they endorse are, of course, the easiest way to describe them in these data. But our theory of factions suggests that at least those that persist might have something in common beyond adherence to a single candidate. The Bernie Sanders supporters are the most obvious candidate for a deeper motivation, and we have labeled them "progressives." But the Edwards supporters also might seem to represent a more moderate or "third way" vision of the Democratic Party. Among Republicans, John McCain was often described as a "maverick" who bucked his own party, but he bucked it from a particular direction. The New York group would seem to be backing local favorite sons, but there is a characterization of East Coast Republicans as particularly concerned with law and order and breaking with their party on issues like gay rights and abortion.

While both parties are divided between establishment and faction, that division manifests in different ways. For one, the Democratic network has nearly twice as many endorsers as the Republican network. Remembering that endorsers can only be included in the network if they endorse in more than one contest, this means that a much smaller number of people repeatedly issue Republican endorsements than issue Democratic ones. This might indicate greater gatekeeping or hierarchy within the Republican Party, as well as a broad-based coalition in the Democratic Party.

The Republican network is slightly denser and less modular than the Democratic network, yet the Republican network also has over twice as many communities (10 to the Democrats' four). This could indicate that the divisions within the Democratic network, though fewer, run deeper. Indeed, the four Democratic communities have distinct endorsement patterns that rarely overlap (more about this in Section Five). Many of the Republican communities overlap in some contests despite having distinct endorsement patterns overall. For example, both the Post-Bush Establishment and the Old Guard mostly endorsed Romney in 2008, but they diverged in other contests. In contrast, the Edwards community does not overlap with the other communities.

One interpretation is that the modern Democratic Party has a large and solid establishment core. Offshoots center around candidates with a different ideological vision (e.g., a more moderate Southern Democratic vision for Edwards, a more progressive vision for Sanders). In contrast, the Republican Party, since the 1990s, has been riddled with different versions of the party establishment, none of whom can quite agree on which candidate should bear the party's standard. The existence of four smaller splinter factions backing markedly more conservative candidates like Huckabee and Cruz shows this as well.

The patterns we observe at the network level seem to support the idea that the Democratic Party is more unified while the Republican Party is increasingly fractured. This tracks the empirical realities of Republican nomination contests in the twenty-first century, as well as the two parties' fortunes in recent legislative leadership battles. The Democratic Party has shown far more unity than the Republicans in selecting a Speaker of the House, for instance.

4.4 Endorser-Level Characteristics

The communities we identify are the sum of their members. To understand how they reflect factional behavior, we look at the actors who make up the factions. How do the people in one community differ from another, if at all?

4.4.1 Ideological Differences

One natural way that politicians might differ is in their ideology. Our conception of ideology is necessarily general here, particularly given the difficulty in measurement. At its most basic, ideology is usually conceptualized in political science as some kind of structure over a political actor's preferences. Typically, scholars imagine that structure as an ideological spectrum or dimension, perhaps ranging from "liberal" to "conservative." But ideological structure might be more complicated, so that one or even two dimensions cannot completely capture it. Meanwhile, the patterns that we use to infer ideology, for example, roll call votes, are of course the function of so many other things (Lee 2010) that disentangling ideology from the rest of it may be futile.

Fortunately for our purposes, it does not matter much what explains ideology, only that our measures capture some kind of structure in preferences. That structure might be liberalism versus conservatism, and that is how we will usually interpret it. But it might also reflect, for example, the conflict over the terms of the coalition, particularly willingness to compromise, as described in Section 2. Or it might reflect something else.

We employ two measures of ideology, each of which has two parts. First, we use the most common measure, DW-NOMINATE (Poole and Rosenthal 1991).[13] This measure summarizes roll call voting in the U.S. Congress with two ideological dimensions, and we'll use both dimensions in this analysis. However, this measure is only available for politicians who have served in Congress. As is summarized in Table 7, some communities have fewer

---

[13] NOMINATE locates each member in a two-dimensional space according to a model that uses that space to predicts their votes. Members who vote together have similar scores. Scholars then interpret this space on the basis of the content of the bills and the location of the members.

Table 7 Ideology score coverage across communities in both networks.

Community name	Has DW-NOM?	Has CF-recipient?	Has CF-contributor?	N
Democratic network				
Cold War Establishment	124 (46%)	155 (57%)	45 (17%)	270
Modern Establishment	246 (56%)	262 (60%)	164 (37%)	440
Edwards Backers	16 (13%)	75 (60%)	40 (32%)	126
Progressives	2 (5.4%)	16 (43%)	11 (30%)	37
Democratic Endorser Total	288 (33%)	508 (58%)	260 (30%)	873
Republican network				
Reagan-Era Establishment	30 (47%)	31 (48.4%)	11 (17.2%)	64
Bush-Era Establishment	102 (58%)	148 (84.6%)	71 (40.6%)	175
Post-Bush Establishment	24 (34%)	57 (81.4%)	31 (39%)	70
Old Guard	23 (70%)	25 (75.8%)	15 (45.5%)	33
East Coast Republicans	4 (13%)	24 (77.4%)	3 (12.5%)	31
Mavericks	12 (24.5%)	34 (68.4%)	13 (26.5%)	49
Republican Endorser Total	217 (51.4%)	341 (80.8%)	190 (45%)	422

members of Congress (this is itself an interesting variation, which we return to in the next section).

A second measure is DIME or campaign finance (CF) scores, based on campaign contributions (Bonica 2023).[14] Here, there are measures for both campaign contributors and campaign donation recipients between 1979 and 2020. Since many of our endorsers have received or donated to a political campaign, we have more coverage of them on this measure.

---

[14] CF scores estimate politician's ideology according to their incoming and outgoing political donations. Politicians with similar donation patterns will have similar scores.

Both these measures place politicians on an ideological scale. The first dimension of DW-NOMINATE and both the contributor and recipient DIME scores are generally interpreted as measuring liberal-to-conservative ideology, as they are understood in the United States. For these three measures, the liberal position is the negative end of the spectrum, and the conservative position is the positive end, so from left to right on the number line. Scores closer to the middle are more moderate, and all these values are relative to one another. The second dimension of NOMINATE is slightly different, as we will discuss later in this section.

Together, the measures reveal a consistent picture of the ideological divides in both parties. Figures 9, 10, 11, and 12 show the four ideological measures for both parties (we use the average score for those whose scores change over the period they are in the data). Each community is labeled with its mean, which is indicated with a vertical white line.

Setting aside the second dimension of DW-NOMINATE, the other three measures show that the establishment communities in both parties tend to be in the same place.

We want to treat the "establishment" groups of each party as the point of comparison. The establishment in both parties shows some slight evidence of the increasing polarization of the parties in this period.

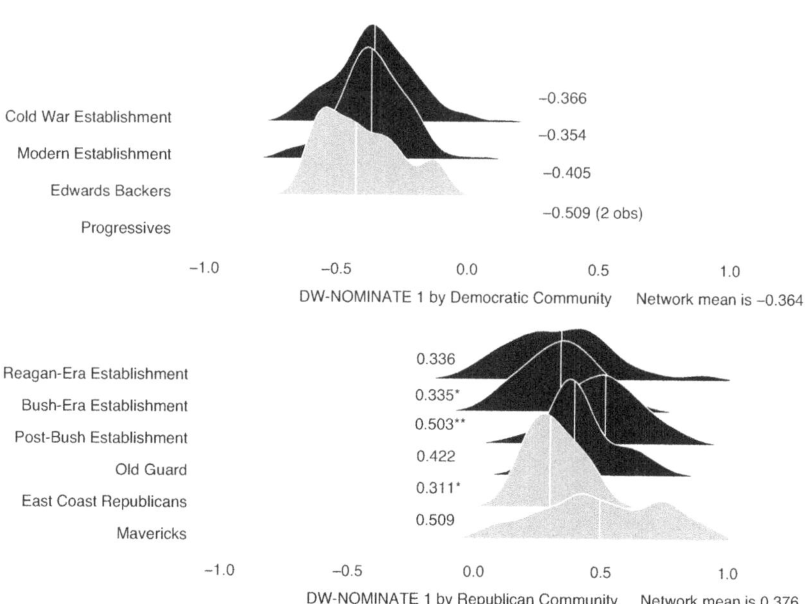

Figure 9 DW-NOMINATE 1st Dimension by party and community.

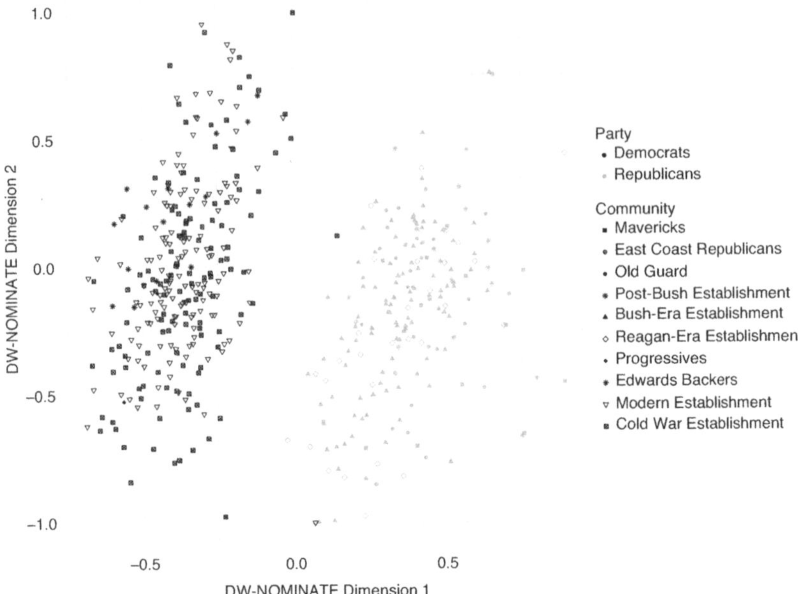

Figure 10 Scatter plot of both dimensions of DW-NOMINATE by party and community.

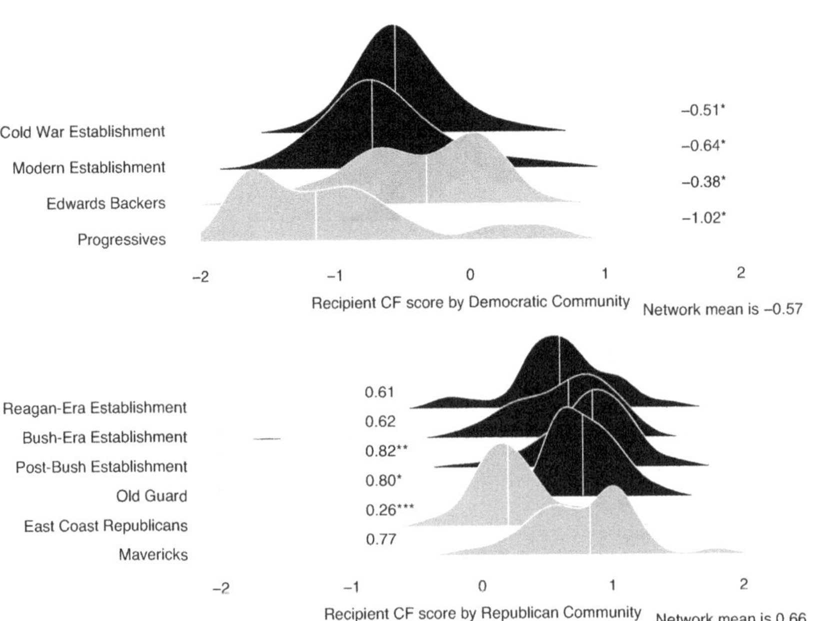

Figure 11 Campaign donation recipient scores by party and community.

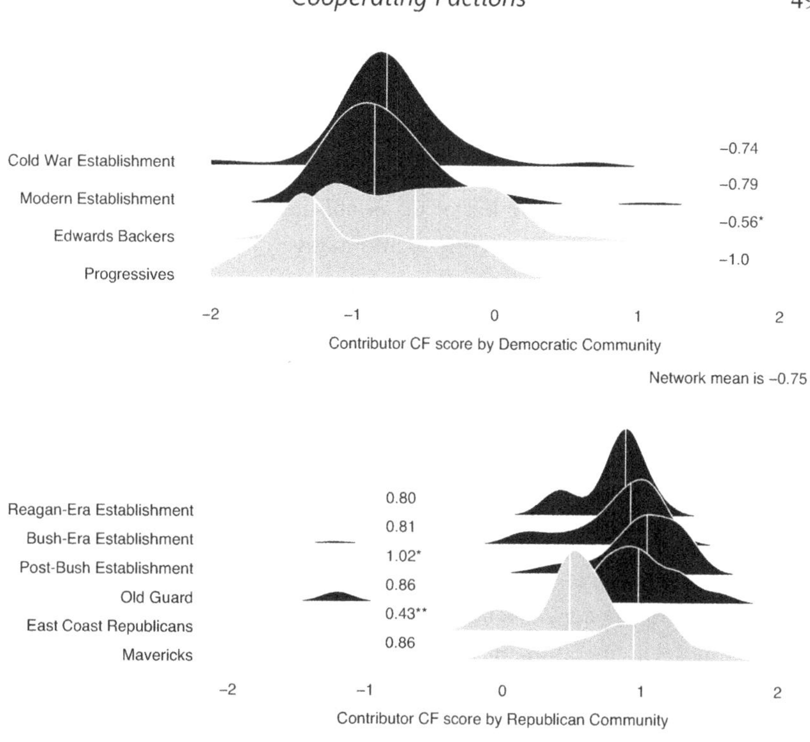

Figure 12 Campaign donation donor scores by party and community.

Among Democrats, there is a barely perceptible shift to the left from the Cold War Establishment to the Modern Establishment. For NOMINATE, the two communities have indistinguishable means (-0.36 vs. -0.37), but the DIME scores, for which we have more observations, show a modest shift (from a mean of -0.51 to -0.64 [$p < 0.000$] for the recipient score and from -0.74 to -0.79 for the donor score). So, the two communities we are calling the establishment stake out the middle of the party. Meanwhile, for Republicans, the establishment is in four communities, three of which succeed each other, the Reagan-Era, Bush-Era, and Post-Bush-Era. These show a steady but again modest shift to the right (with means changing from 0.336 to 0.335 [$p = 0.001$] and then to 0.50 [$p < 0.000$] for NOMINATE, and from 0.61 to 0.62 to 0.82 [$p < 0.000$] for the recipient score and from 0.80 to 0.81 to 1.02 [$p = 0.001$] for the donor score). The other Republican establishment community, the Old Guard, is consistently nestled between the Bush-Era and Post-Bush Establishment communities.

The non-establishment communities are also interesting. Among the Democrats, for both DIME scores, the Progressive/Bernie Sanders community is, as expected, systematically aligned to the left. And the Edwards community is generally just to the right of the establishment. There are only two

Progressives in Congress and only sixteen from the Edwards community, so it is hard to draw much from their NOMINATE scores. The two Progressives do have more liberal NOMINATE scores than the main communities (−0.57 and −0.45). The Edwards community members who served in Congress, though few, are also clustered to the left of the establishment, but the DIME scores, based on more data, are probably more informative.

We interpret this as evidence of two break-away communities that have different ideas of what the party should look like. Both the more centrist Edwards Backers and the more liberal Progressives could be seen as a reaction to the position of the Modern Establishment. Meanwhile, most of the party is supporting the compromise of the eventual nominee.

Among Republicans, we can look for the same phenomenon. We do find it with the East Coast Republicans, who are consistently less conservative than the rest of the party. The Mavericks the Mavericks have a much wider ideological range, but their mean is to the right.

The second dimension of NOMINATE is different from the other measures. It does not measure liberal-to-conservative ideology, and there is not much consensus on what it does measure. Mathematically, it captures whatever structure it can that the first dimension did not capture. Most scholars would argue that, in the twenty-first century at least, it captures something of an insider-outsider or party loyalty dimension, so that lower values are those who will often break from their party's agenda (Duck-Mayr and Montgomery 2023, see also Hussey 2008). In earlier periods, the second dimension has captured regional differences or differences in racial politics. During the mid to late twentieth century, some argued (Poole and Rosenthal 1997, 2007; Noel 2013) a partisan factor and an ideological factor combined to create the two dimensions, but neither dimension perfectly captured only one of those factors. On that interpretation, the liberal-to-conservative axis runs roughly from the southwest to the northeast quadrant of the space, while the partisan dimension is roughly orthogonal, from the northwest to the southeast. This interpretation anchored the so-called "three-party system" of the 1950s and 1960s (Poole and Rosenthal 1997, pp. 45–46, 2007, pp. 54–55), in which Southern Democrats often broke with their party on not only race but other cultural issues. It may have lasted into the 1990s, when Democrats with high scores were often southern and more conservative.

The simple party-loyalty interpretation of the second dimension probably applies to the later years in the data, which is also the period when we have the most competing communities or factions. So, for our purposes, we will treat the second dimension as at least capturing something beyond ideology, and likely loyalty to the party, but with awareness of other options.

It is hard to interpret the second dimension without the first, so Figure 10 adds the second dimension to the first in a scatter plot. It shows that some of our non-establishment communities break with the rest of their party. The Edwards Backers in the Democratic Party are among the most party loyal if we were to follow that interpretation. They are also often from southern states and represent a more culturally conservative wing of the party.

Among Republicans, the four establishment communities are in the middle, but the Post-Bush Establishment has the highest second-dimension score, suggesting they anchor the most loyal part of the party. Meanwhile, both the Mavericks and especially the East Coast Republicans have lower scores, suggesting they are more willing to break with their party.

In sum, we see some ideological distinctions between the smaller, candidate-focused communities in each party, while the main, establishment communities show little ideological variation beyond a slight polarizing trend. We now turn to other reasons that members of the same party might join into subgroups.

4.4.2 State and Regional Differences

After political differences, perhaps the next most natural source of intra-party conflict is region. Geographic differences have long been something that parties struggle to overcome, and geographic representation is hard-wired into the constitutional framework. Presidential nominations are sought across a series of state-level contests, where local differences may be likely to emerge. On the other hand, contemporary politics is increasingly national (Hopkins 2016), and party leaders have an incentive to bridge those differences. Party leaders from across the country all want to find a consensus candidate who can win in the general election.

For this reason, from one "establishment" community to the next, we expect little in geographic variation. We might expect more from early contest states, like New Hampshire and Iowa, and from states where the party is strong. Red states should be overrepresented in the Republican network in general. We should see a similar pattern with blue states and the Democrats. Swing states should matter for both parties, and high-population states are highly represented everywhere. All those patterns are expected in all the establishment communities.

The candidate-centered communities might be different, however. We would expect support to be concentrated in the candidates' home states, for example. That would be consistent with the view that certain network divisions are as much a function of heightened support for specific candidates as of deep ideological differences.

These expectations are mostly met in the data. Figures 13 and 14 show the geographic distribution of endorsers for each community. There, the states shaded in the darkest color have the most endorsers. States with no shading have no endorsers. Early primary states are common across all networks, and there are few differences among the establishment communities within each party network.

Among Democrats, the Cold War Establishment does somewhat depart from that expectation. There, the most represented states are neither early caucus states nor southern states, which were strong in the Democratic Party at least at the beginning of the community's tenure. The community is heavily represented in the most populated blue states: New York and California. The remaining endorsers are dispersed among a variety of states on the Eastern Seaboard, in the Midwest, and in the South. Few endorsers in this community hail from the Mountain West. The Modern Establishment is dominated by endorsers from New Hampshire and three of the most populated states – California, Texas, and New York. Modern Establishment endorsers also represented recent or growing battleground states, like Florida and Georgia, along with states in the Mountain West to a greater extent than did endorsers from other communities. Overall,

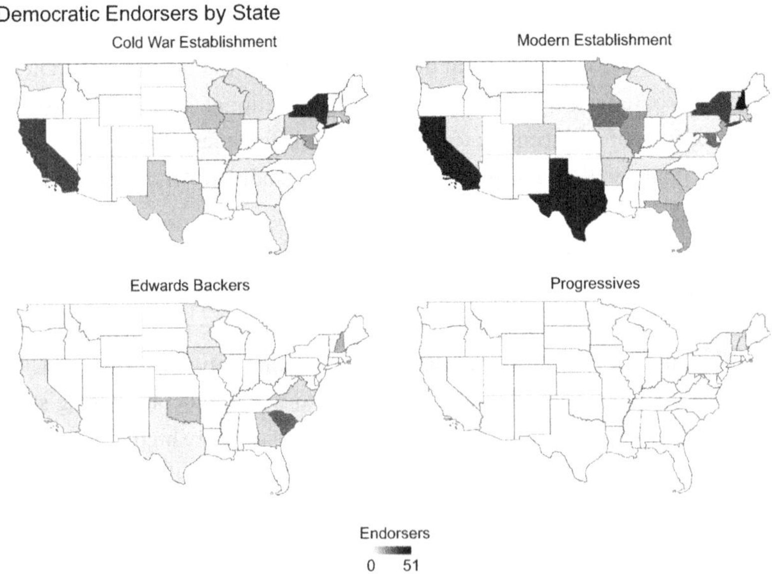

Figure 13 Endorsers in the Cold War and Modern Establishment communities hail from high-population and early caucus states, with shifts reflecting change in caucus order and in battleground state status. Endorsers in the other two communities represent fewer states, including some early contest states.

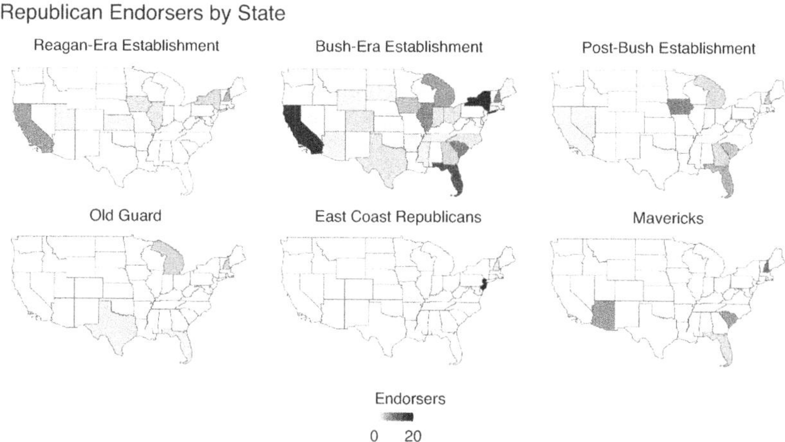

Figure 14 The establishment Republican communities have similar geographic patterns, with an emphasis on early primary states and large population states. The East Coast Republicans have the least geographic diversity.

both establishment communities reflect the geographic diversity of the party at different points in time.

For Republicans, the same is true. Endorsers in the Reagan-Era Establishment are spread out across the country. Reagan's home state of California has the most endorsers (eight), followed by New Hampshire and New York. The remaining endorsers cover territory from Minnesota to Mississippi. Larger concentrations of the Bush-Era Establishment are in large states like New York and California. Clusters are also found in early primary states like New Hampshire and South Carolina, as well as the emerging battleground state of Florida. That continues with the Post-Bush Establishment, with the addition of a greater representation of endorsers from Iowa. The smallest Republican establishment community, the Old Guard, bridges the Bush and Post-Bush communities. Their endorsers are, again, dispersed across states and regions, with the largest numbers in Michigan and New Hampshire (five endorsers in each state), followed by Florida and Texas.

Some of the candidate-focused communities do have a distinct geographic character. Among Democrats, we might expect supporters of John Edwards to be more concentrated in southern states near his home state of North Carolina, and they do. Support for Edwards is especially strong in the early contest state of South Carolina (28 endorsers hail from that state alone). The Progressive/ Sanders community has eight endorsers each from the senator's home state of Vermont and from the neighboring early primary state of New Hampshire.

Among Republicans, the East Coast Republicans are geographically concentrated. Most endorsers in this community – twenty out of thirty-one – hail from

New Jersey. That this community focuses on candidates (e.g., Giuliani, Christie) from this region and that most of its endorsers are from this region, suggests that this community might be a regional subgroup devoted to specific candidates at a specific time.

The Mavericks, in contrast, are more spread out. McCain's home state of Arizona is well-represented, but not as much as the early primary state of New Hampshire. Another early primary state, South Carolina, is also notable. The Mavericks are more involved in mainstream early primary contests than the East Coast Republicans.

These geographic differences further help us distinguish the non-establishment communities. Factional candidates not only draw a lot of support from their home states, but they also have a greater need for early primary wins, because they cannot count on the establishment to prop them up if they stumble early.

4.4.3 Demographic Differences

Intra-party divisions might be driven by demographic characteristics, such as race, age, and gender. While we do not have reliable data on the racial or ethnic identities of the endorsers, we do have their gender and birth year.

Gender does not appear to be a dominant factor in determining communities in either party, although it does track with some of the divisions, particularly among Republicans.

The biggest gender difference is between the parties, not within them. The endorsers in both parties are overwhelmingly male, in keeping with the well-known gender imbalance in U.S. elected offices. But the Democrats have almost twice as many women. Figure 15 shows the gender breakdown for both parties.

Among Democrats, gender does little to distinguish the more recent communities from one another. The Cold War Era Establishment is only 6.6 percent women, but all three more recent communities are between 20 and 25 percent women. The over-time change tracks the modest progress women have made in access to politics.

Among Republicans, there is more variation. The establishment communities have between 3.2 percent (Reagan-Era) and 12.1 percent (Bush-Era) women, but just less than one-fifth of the East Coast Republicans are women, and about 14.3 percent of the McCain community is. While no one community is characterized by being predominantly women, most of the establishment communities are characterized by being extremely male. At most, then, the outsider or challenger communities are more gender diverse.

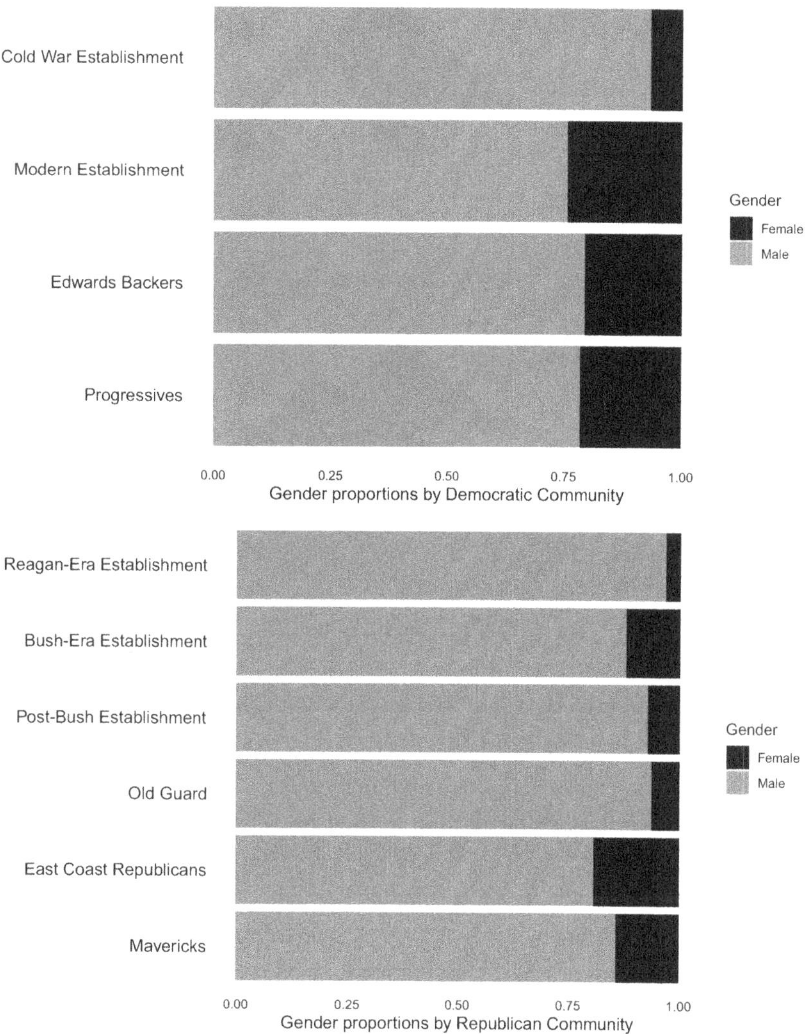

Figure 15 Shaded bars show the proportion of males and females in endorsement communities by party.

We make a similar observation about the generational differences among the communities. At least some of the outsider communities have more members of younger generations. Figure 16 shows the age distribution, based on the birth year of each community's endorsers, per community.

We have noted before that the establishment communities seem divided in time. The pool of endorsers in one era gives way to a newer pool in later eras. This naturally tracks their ages. The Cold War Establishment is the oldest community in the Democratic Party. Birth years range from 1903 to 1965,

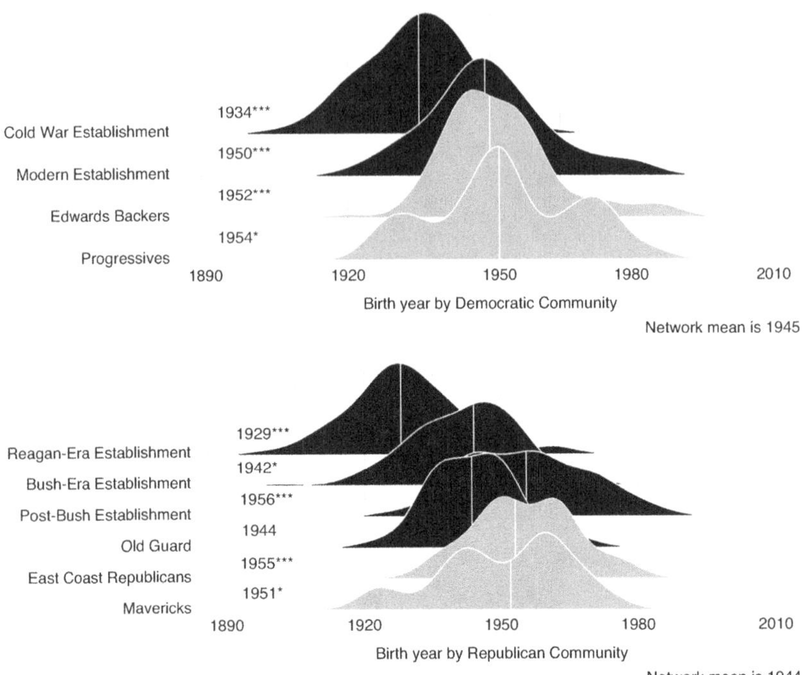

Figure 16 Age cohort by party and community.

with the average endorser in this community born in 1934. For the Modern Establishment, birth years range from 1918 to 1987, with a mean birth year of 1950.

The same changeover can be seen in the Republican Party. Endorsers in the Reagan-Era Establishment community were born between 1900 and 1962 with an average birth year of 1928. The community with the next earliest birth years is the Bush-Era Establishment, with birth years between 1902 to 1972, with an average of 1942. The Post-Bush Establishment has the youngest endorsers in the network, with birth years ranging from 1927 to 1983, with a mean of 1956. The Old Guard bridges the last two communities, with an average birth year of 1944, and a range from 1924 to 1967.

In addition to the general replacement of one generation with the next, some of the outsider communities also include younger members. The Progressive Community among the Democrats has a large mode of the younger generation. The Mavericks also include a good number of younger endorsers, and the East Coast Republicans are consistently younger than the rest of the Republican Party.

These age differences track a recurring tendency for intra-party conflict to be generational (Beck 1984; Miroff 2009; Munger 2022; McSweeney n.d.). Those generational differences may follow policy differences, or just a desire for a new cohort to capture the reins of the party from the past.

4.4.4 Different Roles in the Party

Finally, we look at the different roles that endorsers play in the party when they are not directly participating in nomination politics. We conceptualize the range of party roles in two ways. First, we examine the level of office held by endorsers within each community, including national, state, local, party, or no office. Second, we use a slightly adapted version of the endorser weighting index from Cohen et al. 2008 to assign endorsers a weight corresponding with their influence in the party. Weights range from zero (e.g., an attorney with no long-standing political ties) to one (e.g., a sitting president). A full version of this index can be found in Section 2, Table 3. Finally, we compare the relative connectedness of each community to the party network overall using betweenness and closeness centrality.

Figure 17 shows the proportion of each community's endorsers who *ever held* national, state, local, party, or no office. We recorded the office held by each endorser at the time that they made each endorsement. We also recorded previous offices held by endorsers. Since all endorsers in our network endorse at least twice, we have two or more independent observations of office per endorser. Some endorsers remain in the same office, while others move to a higher or lower office over time. This means that one endorser could potentially be coded as holding more than one office, so the percentages in Figure 17 will sum to more than 100 percent. An endorser coded as none is one who has never held any office.

The biggest difference that emerges from Figure 17 is between those who ever held a national office and those who ever held a state office. The candidate-centered communities in both parties are dominated by state office holders (e.g., state legislators), and local office holders (e.g., mayors) are more common in those communities as well. The more establishment communities, on the other hand, are where most national figures are found.

This is especially true for the Old Guard community in the Republican Party, which is almost entirely national figures, we think marking them as particularly establishment.

The office holder patterns suggest three things about both parties' endorsement networks, and thus about the parties. Assuming that national office holders have relatively more influence in the party, the balance of power is tilted toward

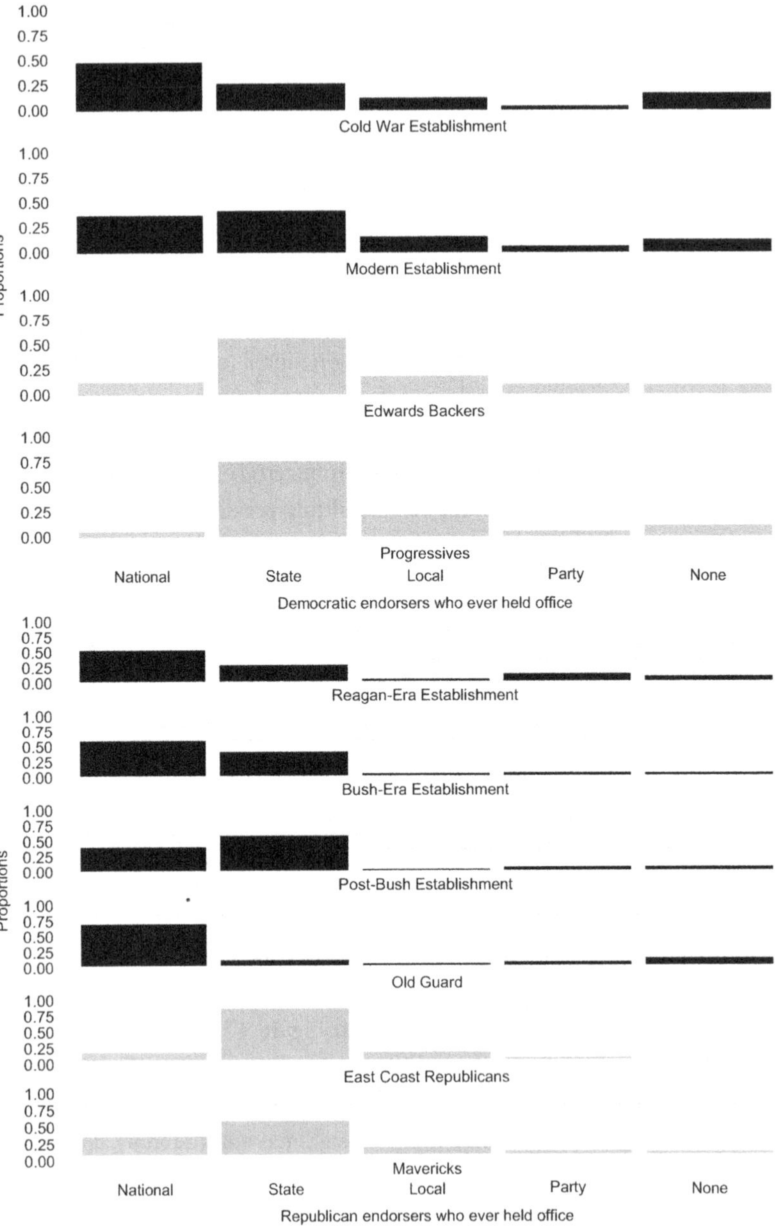

Figure 17 The type of officeholder varies by community, with a greater proportion of national officeholders in the establishment communities, and a greater proportion of state office holders in the candidate-centered communities.

the establishment communities. Second, and incorporating insights from the state maps, the candidate-centered communities seem to be dominated by state and local officials from a few states that are especially receptive to these candidates, consistent with an insurgent strategy. Finally, it adds depth to the generational story we told in the previous section, given that for many, political careers begin at the local level and move up as they become more successful.

There are also meaningful differences between the parties on this dimension. Figure 18 shows that the Republican network skews toward national office holders, followed by state office holders. There is little representation from other levels of the party, including local office holders, party office holders, and non-office holders. In the Democratic network, state officeholders outnumber national officeholders, and other members of the party, especially local and non-office holders, are represented in higher proportions.

There is less repeat input from lower-office holders in the Republican Party. The party may be more hierarchical, or local officials may be less interested in engaging with presidential politics. It may be that the Republican Party has become more nationalized more quickly, relative to the Democratic Party.

The national versus state divisions are important since U.S. parties mimic the federal structure of the country. But there is also variation within these levels.

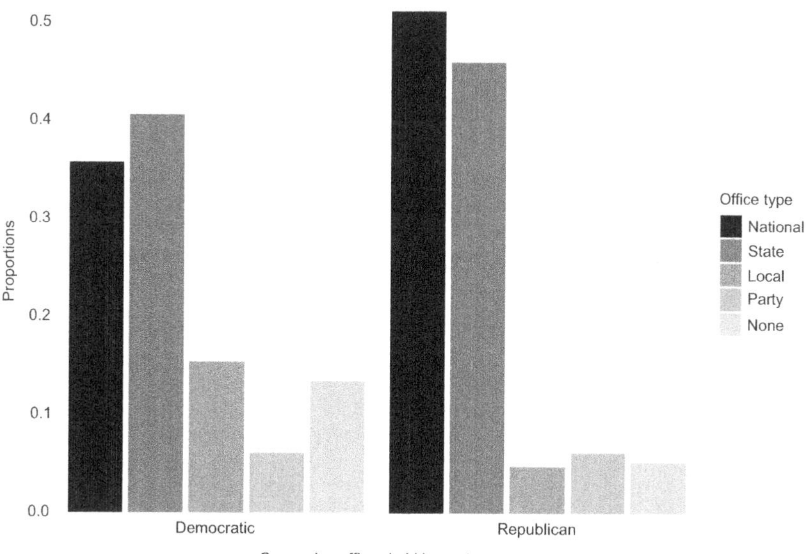

Figure 18 The Democratic network has more representation from different offices, while the Republican network is dominated by higher-level office holders.

A Governor, for example, is a state official, but might have a larger platform than a first-term U.S. House member. We capture this variation by weighting each endorser based on the exact office they hold at the time of each endorsement. We then average the weight scores by the endorser. For example, one endorser might make their first endorsement as a member of a state legislature (weight of 0.2), their second as a U.S. House member (weight of 0.4), and their third as a U.S. Senator (weight of 0.6). This individual would have a combined weight of 0.4.[15]

Figure 19 shows the distribution of each endorser's average weight by community. Higher-weighted members are presumed to be more influential in the party. Again, we see the pattern whereby the candidate communities have a lower average weight. For the Edwards Backers, the mean weight is 0.23, and for the Progressives, it is 0.21. A disconnected right tail in the Edwards Backers Distribution stems from endorsements by former president Jimmy Carter,

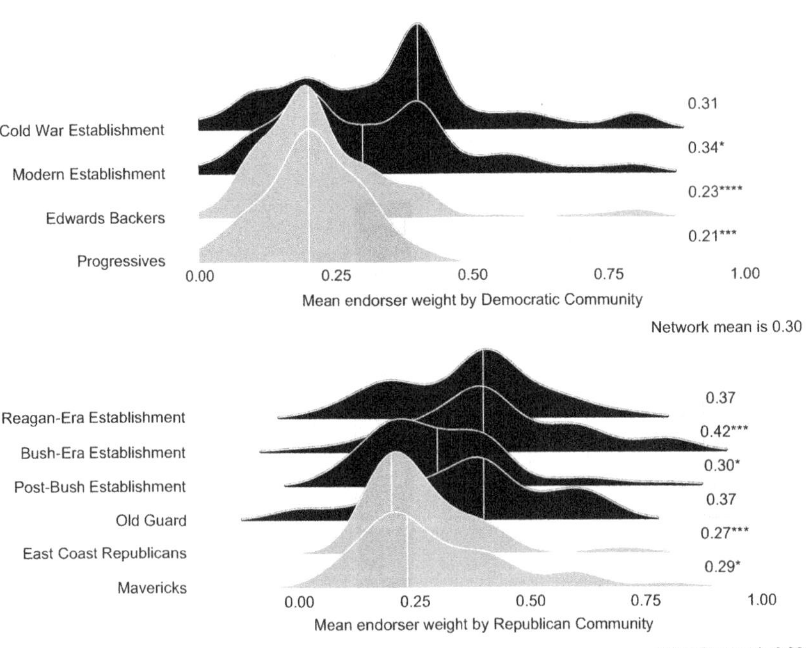

Figure 19 Mean endorser weight for communities within both parties. The establishment communities have more high-weight endorsers than the candidate communities, with some variation.

---

[15] For a full description of the weighting scheme, see Section 2, Table 3.

national unions like the AFL-CIO, and several governors. The McCain community has a mean of 0.29, and the East Coast Republicans are at 0.27.

The between-party difference is present for this measure as well. The median Republican endorser has a weight of 0.4 (e.g., a sitting member of the U.S. House), and a mean of 0.36. The median Democratic endorser, in contrast, has a median and a mean weight of 0.30 (e.g., a member of the DNC, a mayor of a medium-large city).

Network centrality provides another way to understand the differing party roles of endorsers (and communities). Unlike mean weight and office held, which incorporate outside information, network centrality measures reflect only the position of each actor in the network. It offers another angle on the relative nature of the communities. Are "important" endorsers also positioned in important places in the network? For example, a community that had a higher relative betweenness than mean weight would contain well-connected endorsers, even if those endorsers weren't high-level office holders.

We report centrality statistics for Democrats in Figure 20, which contains two panes. The top pane shows the distribution of network-level betweenness for the

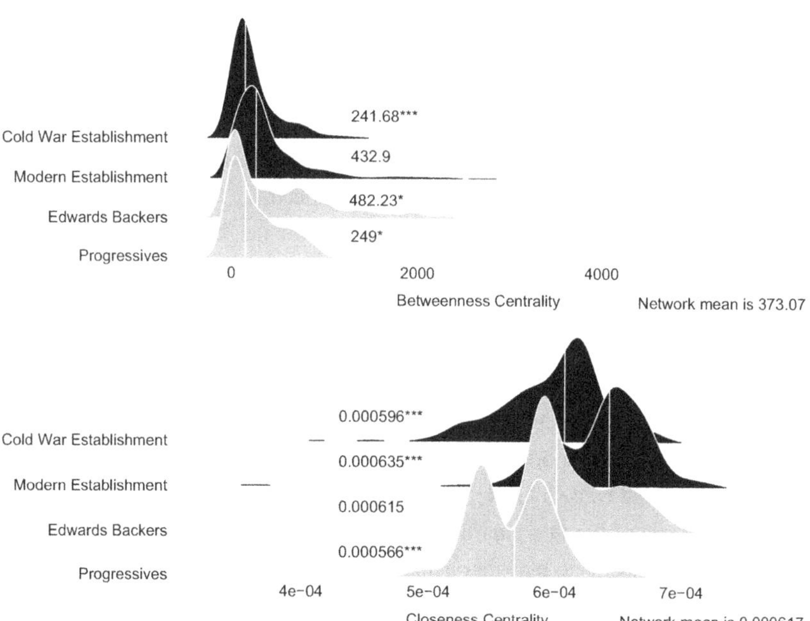

Figure 20 The mean for each community is labeled on the figure ($*p < 0.05$, $**p < 0.001$, $***p < 0.000$, for the difference between the community mean and the party network mean).

Democratic communities, and the bottom shows closeness. The means are indicated with white vertical lines in the distributions and are also printed on the plot, as are indicators of each community's mean centrality is statistically different than the network's mean (373.07 for betweenness, 0.000617 for closeness).

The Edwards Backers have the highest mean betweenness score followed by the Modern Establishment, the Progressives, and the Cold War Establishment. As with betweenness, the two communities with the highest average closeness scores are the Edwards Backers and the Modern Establishment. This time, the Modern Establishment comes out on top, followed by the Edwards Backers, the Cold War Establishment, and the Progressives with a mean of 0.000566.

These patterns differ in some ways from what we have observed using other measures of role in the party (e.g., mean weight, office held). The fact that the Edwards Backers lead with betweenness scores suggests that endorsers in this community are well-connected in the network overall. We detect a distinct community, but that community's members are not far from the rest of the network. Major national unions and political figures (e.g., Jimmy Carter) are part of this community. That the Modern Establishment is also made up of well-connected endorsers is not surprising, but the fact that the Progressives community edges out the Cold War community in terms of betweenness is.[16] This suggests that the two candidate-centered communities are not complete silos but are instead home to well-connected actors. The low ranking of the Cold War Establishment suggests differences between the older version of the party and the newer version. The slight divergence in betweenness and closeness rankings signals that the influence of each community in the party is somewhat nuanced.

We show the distribution of centrality scores for the Republican network in Figure 21. As in Figure 20, we test differences with the party's mean centrality (194.56 for betweenness, 0.00124 for closeness).

The community rankings are nearly identical using both measures of centrality, with one exception. The Old Guard has the highest scores for betweenness, while the Bush-Era Establishment has the highest scores for closeness. After that, the ranking is, in descending order: Mavericks, Post-Bush Establishment, Reagan-Era Establishment, and East-Coast Republicans. One of the most interesting takeaways is the high score of the Old Guard. This small community, bridging the pre- and Post-Bush Eras, seems to play an outsize role in connecting the network.

Overall, the betweenness and closeness rankings for the Republican communities overlap more with one another, and with the mean weight rankings, than do

---

[16] The two candidate-centered communities have higher minimum scores than the establishment communities (13.44 for Edwards Backers and 9.00 for the Progressives as opposed to a minimum of zero for both establishment communities), but the Modern Establishment has the highest maximum score.

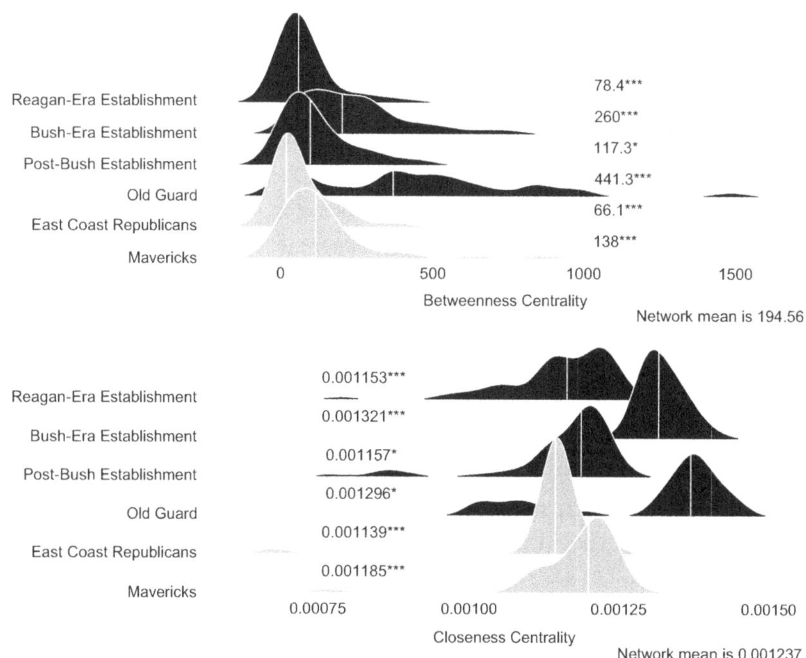

Figure 21 The mean for each community is labeled on the figure ($*p < 0.05$, $**p < 0.001$, $***p < 0.000$, for the difference between the community mean and the party network mean).

those for the Democrats. This suggests that the candidate-centered communities are more at the fringes of the Republican network than they are of the Democratic one.

4.5 Comparing the Two Endorsement Networks

At the outset of this section, we set up the question of whether the parties were similar or not, and if not, in what way.

Broadly speaking, we paint similar pictures for the two parties. Both parties have dominant "establishment" communities, which replace one another over time. And both parties have a few more minor communities that break with the establishment, mostly to the benefit of specific candidates. Those minor communities share a similar relationship to the establishment in both parties. They are defined in large part because of their support for specific candidates, but they also have some systematic ideological differences. They tend to be made up of less powerful, younger, state- and local-level officials.

Considering our discussion of factions in Section 2, these two non-establishment groups seem to show the markers of all the different reasons that factions might emerge. Maybe they have different visions for the party.

Maybe they are just loyal to different people. They are generally short-lived, although some of the significant communities are new, so we do not know how long they will persist. They are also relatively small, compared to the establishment communities. The idea that the parties are split into two (or more) clusters of equal influence is not well-supported.

Instead, the dominant conflict seems to be between the establishment – actors who are interested in coordinating – and one or another smaller insurgent factions, trying to overcome that establishment. Less Civil War than Shays' Rebellion.

We don't think these communities are factions *per se*, but they are the result of factional behavior. There are divisions within the parties, but when it comes time to choose a nominee, potential nominees work to consolidate support from across those divisions.

This section's systematic review of the Democratic and Republican endorsement patterns reveals that, at least in the arena of presidential nominating politics, the two parties differ from one another in some fundamental ways some of which may be ripe for further investigation.

The Republican endorsers come from a narrow swathe of the party that overrepresents males who hold higher-level offices. This is consistent with the idea that the Republican Party is a more hierarchical organization. Hierarchy does not, however, mean unity. The contemporary Republican Party is characterized by a lack of consensus on who should lead the party, which could be interpreted as a lack of consensus on what the party is.

In contrast, the Democrats attract a greater number of endorsers who represent a variety of offices. Despite their varying backgrounds, these endorsers tend to coordinate around nominees to a much greater extent than do the Republicans. This aligns with the idea that the Democratic coalition is less hierarchical. Despite this, the Democratic coalition appears more unified on what the party is, and who should represent it. Democratic endorsers appear to be falling in line, not falling in love.

5 Lanes

Contemporary media coverage of factions in presidential nominations often uses the metaphor of "lanes" (Berkowitz 2015; Bump 2015; Devega 2016; Wilson 2016; McLaughlin 2019; Scott 2019; Martin and Epstein 2019). In the 2020 Democratic nomination race, for example, pundits discussed an "establishment" or "centrist" lane, occupied by candidates like Joe Biden, Amy Klobuchar, and Pete Buttigieg, and a "progressive" or "ideological" lane, occupied by candidates like Bernie Sanders and Elizabeth Warren. To complicate matters, different commentators identify different possible lanes, sometimes two, sometimes a handful. While some candidates might try to straddle more than one lane, or else make their own path, the idea is that winning the nomination requires candidates to pick a lane.

This notion of lanes implies two things. First, candidates have a core appeal to an existing set of supporters within the party, and second, that only one candidate can succeed for each such group of supporters. If Sanders and Warren are competing in the progressive lane, then they are fighting over the same limited set of progressive supporters. To win, a candidate must become the best standard-bearer for a particular lane and use that lane's support to make it to later contests.

The language of lanes connects directly to our idea of factions and our idea of strategic behavior in nominations, which we discussed in Section 2. There, we outlined various notions of factions. A faction could be made up of those who represent a distinct group or groups, those who want a different bargain to be struck among the existing groups, or those who strongly favor a particular political leader. The first two types *could* describe lanes. If the third type describes a lane, it is a narrow one, because it is defined by the people the faction likes. If someone other than Sanders can compete in the Sanders Lane, then it is not the Sanders Lane, it is a progressive lane.

We also argued in Section 2 that factions might not always choose sincerely when backing a candidate. But the logic of lanes suggests that, at least in a limited way, they do. If lanes are the right way to think about nominations, then voters and politicians that make up one lane will only choose from among the candidates competing in that lane. If they choose from across the field, then they are not really defining a lane, and candidates are not really competing in lanes.

Of course, the metaphor of lanes need not be taken so literally. With increasingly large fields of candidates, journalists need some device to organize them. Grouping candidates who seem to have similar appeals is a good start. But winning the nomination requires candidates to go beyond their natural sources of appeal. Lanes are not a good metaphor for coalition-building and faction-bridging behavior.

Instead of multiple paths to the nomination, we suggest there is often only one. Nominees need to unite the support of the many factions in the party. Each party is, in the end, a one-lane highway. That might be particularly true for endorsements. Voters and donors, perhaps, might not be interested in finding a candidate who can unify the party, but at least according to Cohen et al. (2008), party leaders are.

5.1 Are There Lanes in Endorsement Behavior?

Ultimately, the lane metaphor is only as useful as it is empirically accurate. Do we find evidence of lane-like behavior in our endorsement communities?

We showed in Section 4 that the communities we find do not fit perfectly with the expected factions. We instead interpret them as reflecting the process of party leaders strategically choosing and coalescing around a compromise candidate. But perhaps these communities *are* the lanes, and we have been taking the wrong perspective. If we let the data speak, then the clusters of endorsers who have similar nomination preferences might be thought of as lanes.

Since our data cover a fifty-year period, we are describing durable lanes. In any given nomination, are there groups within the party defined by their support in other election cycles that several candidates might compete over in that cycle? If so, we would expect to find each candidate drawing support from one community. On the other hand, if candidates are piecing together their own coalitions, they would draw support from different communities.

Figures 22 and 23 show the distribution of support for all the major candidates in the Democratic and Republican nominations, respectively.

Figure 22 Percent of each candidate's support across Democratic communities.

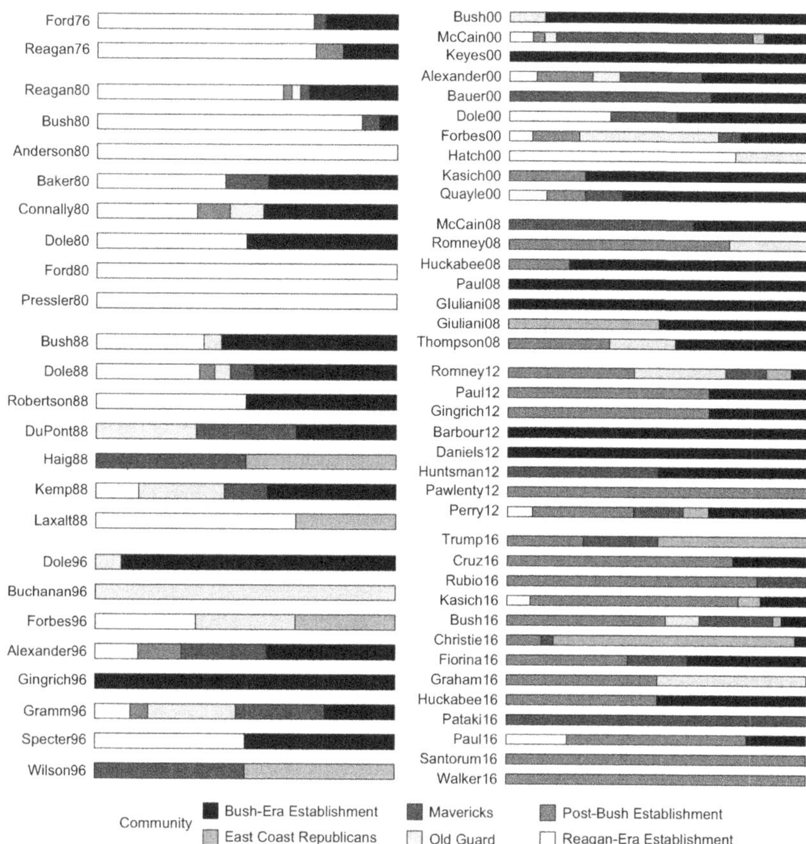

Figure 23 Percent of each candidate's support across Republican communities.

The story from these figures is not primarily one of lanes. Very few successful candidates draw almost all their support from only one community. If there are lanes, they are establishment lanes. We find that some candidates are successful with the lion's share of their support coming from the establishment. and that they tend to share that establishment with others.

The few exceptions fit our interpretations in Section 4. Bernie Sanders does draw largely from one community, the community defined by its support for him. But Elizabeth Warren, often described as a rival for progressive support, draws far more support from the establishment community that also backed Biden and others.

What is evident in the Democratic races is a changeover between the Cold War Establishment and the Modern Establishment. From the 1980s to the early 2000s, the tail end of the older establishment is slowly displaced by the newer one. But there does not appear to be competition between those communities, as with an old-school lane and a new-emerging lane.

Among Republicans, we observe an ever-wider breadth of support. Mitt Romney, the nominee in 2012, draws from five different communities. John McCain, the nominee in 2008, had significant support from the establishment in 2000 and 2008.

We have limited evidence of lanes-like behavior among endorsers. However, Figures 20 and 21 do not take full advantage of the network structure of our data. If the argument is that groups of candidates compete among each other for the same set of support, we would expect to find clusters of candidates, defined by their support from common endorsers.

The endorser-by-endorser projections analyzed in Section 4 identify when endorsers have similar behaviors, not when candidates have similar support. But we can use the candidate-by-candidate projections for that. Figures 2 and 3 in Section 3 show both parts of the network. The candidate-by-candidate projection links candidates through the endorsers they have in common. We again detect communities using the walk-trap algorithm. If candidates are principally competing for the same endorsers within lanes, those communities would be the lanes.

That is not what we find. Table 8 lists the candidates who are in each community we detect (the many minor candidates who are alone in their own community in both parties are omitted). The detected communities do not show deeply divided networks, with modularity scores of 0.161 for the Democratic Party and 0.143 for the Republican Party. In other words, what divisions we do find are not that strong.

The major communities do not look like the collection of candidates who we would think of as being in the same lane. For the Democrats, 2020 rivals Elizabeth Warren and Joe Biden are in the same community (Community 4) with 2008 rivals Hillary Clinton and Barack Obama, and 2004 rivals John Kerry and Howard Dean. Among Republicans, all but two of the eventual nominees are in Community 2, the exceptions being Donald Trump, who heads a tiny lane of outsiders, and Romney in 2012, whose lane does seem to be the kind of candidate contemporary commentators call the traditional, Romney-wing of the party.

There are some patterns among the less successful candidates. Among the Democrats, Communities 2, 3, and 6 each do seem to collect like-minded candidates, with mainstream liberals in Community 2 and moderates in Community 3. And Community 5 clearly fits with the Progressive Community we've identified among the endorsers. But the most consistent similarity is that of time. Candidates from a particular time period tend to be

Table 8 Communities detected in candidate-by-candidate projection for each party.

Democratic candidate communities					
Community 1	**Community 2**	**Community 3**	**Community 4**	**Community 5**	**Community 6**
Clinton 16	Muskie 72	Carter 80	Gore 00	Sanders 20	Mondale 84
Edwards 04	Jackson 88	Gore 88	Clinton 08	Sanders 16	Dukakis 88
Edwards 08	Kennedy 80	Gephardt 88	Obama 08	Kucinich 04	Bradley 00
Harris 20	Humphrey 76	Clinton 92	Richardson 08		Simon 88
Buttigieg 20	Brown 80	Hart 88	Clark 04		Biden 88
Dodd 08	Carter 76	Jackson 76	Kerry 04		Bennet 20
Hickenlooper 20	Bayh 76	Hart 84	Dean 04		Harkin 92
Daschle 04	Harris 76	Askew 84	Warren 20		Schroeder 88
Biden 16	Cranston 84	Glenn 84	Babbitt 88		
Booker 20	Jackson 84	Hollings 84	Gephardt 04		
Klobuchar 20	Bayh 72	Lieberman 04	Biden 20		
Castro 20	Humphrey 72	Jackson 72	Bullock 20		
Ryan 20	Udall 76	McCurdy 92	OMalley 16		
Gillibrand 20	Tsongas 92		Biden 08		
Inslee 20	Sharpton 04		Kerrey 92		
			ORourke 20		
			Delaney 20		
			Foley 88		

Table 8 (cont.)

Republican candidate communities					
Community 1	**Community 2**	**Community 3**	**Community 4**	**Community 5**	**Community 6**
Trump 16	Dole 96	Reagan 76	Bush 16	Paul 16	Gramm 96
Huckabee 16	Ford 76	Haig 88	Romney 08	Paul 12	Kemp 88
Huckabee 08	Bush 00	Laxalt 88	Romney 12		Forbes 96
Fiorina 16	Dole 88		Thompson 08		Barbour 12
Huntsman 12	Alexander 00		Kasich 16		
	Bush 80		Perry 12		
	Bush 88				
	McCain 08				
	Dole 00				
	Baker 80				
	Reagan 80				
	McCain 00	**Community 7**	**Community 8**	**Community 9**	**Community 10**
	Quayle 00	Giuliani 08	Daniels 12	Brownback 08	Buchanan 92
	Hatch 00	Wilson 96	Bauer 00	Santorum 12	Buchanan 96
	Paul 08	Christie 16			
	Connally 80	Kasich 00			
	Alexander 96				

backed by the same set of endorsers. Among Republicans, Community 6 is a more conservative wing, and Community 7 matches what we identified as an East Coast Republican Community among the endorsers.

This pattern follows what we saw in Section 4. There is an establishment that supports almost all the victors as well as most of the mainstream losing candidates. A few small communities do seem to reflect a common appeal, but they are small and short-lived. We do not see evidence of a recurring battle among two or more competing wings of the party. We see some evidence of periodic challenges from distinct candidates against a (typically) successful establishment.

5.2 Are There Lanes in Other Places?

Two features of our data may make it hard to detect lanes. First, we are looking at strategic elites. As we suggested in Section 2, they may not sincerely reveal what side they are on.

From our perspective, this is a feature and not a bug, because it accurately captures how party leaders think about nominations. But if party leaders are not (or are no longer) central to the process, then we are looking in the wrong place. Perhaps voters define lanes, and voters are the ultimate decision makers.

Second, we are looking for patterns across a long period. For us, factions must be enduring. But it is possible that party coalitions are changing much more rapidly than that. Every contest might have new terrain for candidates to navigate.

We can get at both issues by looking at voter preferences. To do so, we need a voter sample that includes questions not just about voters' preferred candidates, but also about alternatives. Most polls do not include this information. It is hard to detect which candidates have overlapping appeals if we only ever observe one choice from each voter. Increasingly, pollsters are asking voters about more than their first choice in nomination contests. One particularly useful survey is the Iowa State University/Civiqs panel conducted in 2019 and 2020.

The Democrats require participants in the Iowa Caucuses to switch their choice if their first-choice candidate does not garner 15 percent of the support in their precinct. Such a candidate is not "viable," and the caucus-goer must choose a candidate who is. This process of "realignment" gives us a unique window into how voters might define lanes. Iowa caucus-goers have an incentive to think about their second choices, and in some cases, will end up formally backing their second choice.

In 2020, the Democratic Party experimented with a balloting format for the Iowa Caucuses that would track each caucus-goer's first and second choice. This increased attention to the first and second choices inspired more attention to this potential switch. We have collected a handful of surveys that ask respondents to provide both their first and second choice. These include the ISU/Civiqs poll's panel survey of potential caucus-goers in the lead-up to the 2020 caucuses. Each subject was surveyed five times before the caucuses, and again once afterward, asking what they did at the caucus. This panel thus provides a rich source of data on the appeal of candidates to Iowans throughout the nomination process. If candidates are competing in lanes, we would expect them to draw from similar supporters.

We also have three other surveys that ask first and second choices. Our 2020 New Hampshire data comes from an exit poll following the New Hampshire primaries, and our Pennsylvania data comes from an online poll of that state's residents, fielded by Civiqs between March and April of 2020 (data from Hopkins and Sigler 2024). Finally, we include a nationally representative sample of Republicans, fielded by YouGov between November 17 and 27, 2023. While Republicans didn't "realign" in the Iowa caucus, some observers expected the "anti-Trump" vote in that year to coalesce around an alternative, and pollsters became more interested in voters' second choices.

As one might expect, in all these cases, many voters are persistent in their support for the same candidate (Peterson 2020). But this survey allows each respondent to name up to twelve different candidates (first and second choices across six waves). To take advantage of that information, we mirror the analysis we have done for endorsements. We create a bipartite network, as described in Section 3, linking respondents and candidates.[17] We then project this into a candidate-by-candidate and a respondent-by-respondent network.

The other data are not quite as rich since they are not a five-wave panel. But we plot similar networks for Democratic voters in New Hampshire and Pennsylvania.

The three panes in Figure 24 show the Iowa, New Hampshire, and Pennsylvania respondents' first and second choices in the 2020 contest.[18] Here, we represent respondents' first and second choices in network form, where the candidates are the nodes. The edges are weighted to correspond to the number of respondents who indicate a pair of candidates as their first and second choices. Candidates connected by thicker lines are those that are

---

[17] We treat each respondent's support for a candidate as a single edge, even if they supported the same candidate more than once.

[18] 508 New Hampshire respondents and 1,336 Pennsylvania respondents listed their first and second Democratic primary choices.

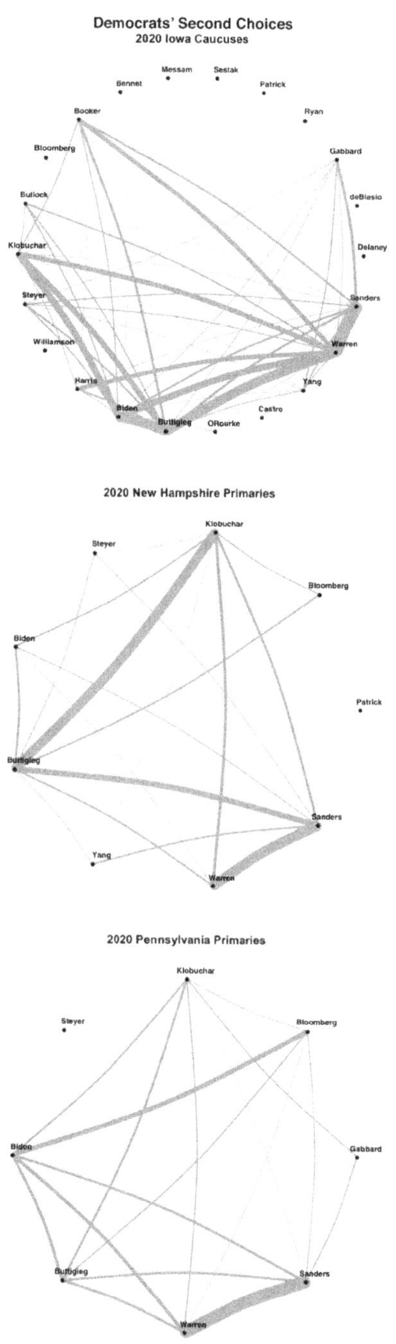

Figure 24 Democratic first and second candidate choices.

more commonly linked as first and second choices, and those connected by thinner lines are those less commonly connected in this way.

In each pane, the candidates are arranged according to their 2020 DIME CF-Recipient scores, which give a rough approximation of the candidates' ideology. The Iowa respondents were asked about twenty-two candidates. This number shrank to nine for New Hampshire and eight for Pennsylvania, as many candidates had dropped out of the race by the time of these contests. We find evidence of some expected patterns, such as between the more progressive candidates Warren and Sanders, but we do not see consistent and exclusive clusters of support. Every candidate shares at least some support with almost every other candidate, and some of the patterns differ by state.

In Iowa, where we have the densest data, progressives Sanders and Elizabeth Warren do have several connections. They are preferred by many voters. But Warren's supporters also back many other candidates, including Pete Buttigieg, Joe Biden, Amy Klobuchar, Kamala Harris, and Cory Booker. Meanwhile, there might be a conservative cluster with Biden, Buttigieg, and Klobuchar, but that triangle is also well-connected to Warren and has more than a few ties to Sanders.

The much thinner New Hampshire network might be interpreted as having two clusters – Sanders/Warren and Buttigieg/Klobuchar – but these are linked by a significant tie between Buttigieg and Sanders, and there are other ties among the four of them.

In Pennsylvania, again, Sanders and Warren have strong ties, but Biden is connected to both, as well as to Bloomberg, Buttigieg, and Klobuchar.

This is broadly consistent with the pattern among the elites. Bernie Sanders does have a distinct appeal, and his supporters are not generally coming from or going to too many others except Elizabeth Warren. But Warren, with the rest of the field, traces out a complicated tangle.

We perform a similar analysis using the data from the 2024 Republican primary contest.[19] We plot the connections between respondents' first and second choices in the Republican primaries in Figure 25. As with Figure 24, the wider lines correspond with more respondents listing a given pair of candidates as their first and second choices. Here, we order the candidates in terms of their affinity toward Trump, based on our understanding of the candidates and their positions, with Chris Christie anchoring the least-Trumpy end of the distribution.

---

[19] 398 respondents in this survey listed their first and second choices for the 2024 Republican primaries.

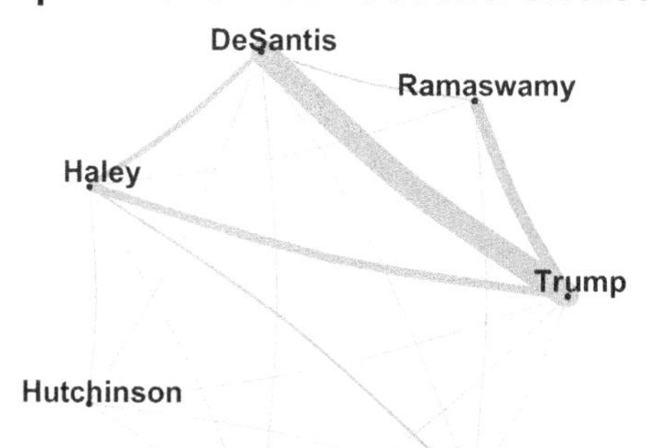

Figure 25 Republican first and second candidate choices.

As with the 2020 Democrats, we see a few patterns, but we also see a lot of shared support. The strongest links are between support for Trump and DeSantis, followed by support for Trump and Ramaswamy. But Haley and Trump also share a strong link, even stronger than the link between Haley and DeSantis. There is not much of a picture of an anti-Trump wing of the party. There are anti-Trump candidates, but their support among voters does not describe much of a "lane."

The lack of definitive, pervasive patterns is ultimately the explanation. Some voters care about the policy or ideologically defined lanes that observers have identified, but these lanes are not always clear, and many voters care about an array of other things. Candidates try to build appeal across a diverse electorate with demographic, attitudinal, and policy differences. Especially in primaries, ideological differences among the candidates are minimal, and other dimensions become salient.

5.3 Are Lanes Useful?

The analysis in this section does not mean that the metaphor of "lanes" should be discarded. For one thing, it very suitably captures the idea of factions. As a first cut at a crowded field, it makes sense to ask which candidates have similar appeals.

On a practical level, it would be worthwhile for political surveys to not only ask these second-choice questions, but also to analyze these patterns. The intuition that candidates draw from competing subgroups within the party is not well supported, at least not among 2020 voters.[20]

---

[20] It also does not seem present in 2016. A YouGov/Huffington Post survey in 2015 and 2016 (see Noel 2016a, 2018) asked first and second choice questions of a national sample of activists.

The idea of lanes also foregrounds the importance of the party as the ground being fought over. It is common to treat presidential nominations from the perspective of those hoping to be chosen, as a contest among candidates, gathering resources and votes. But the party – voters, activists, and officials – are the choosers, and the divisions among them are important. The party is the ground being fought over, and some candidates have more appeal in some areas than others.

But in the end, "lanes" suggest that there are multiple clear paths to the finish, and a candidate just needs to win in their own path. That's not true. Ultimately, a candidate has to win across the entire field. Maybe a better metaphor would be some kind of game where players try to amass territory, like Risk. Two players may find themselves competing for the same continent, but if they focus only on winning their own local area, they won't get far.

Even this metaphor breaks down because it doesn't give the choosers much agency. The party is not just the pavement of the racecourse or the map to be conquered. Its members, politicians, and voters are active participants. The way they participate is through cooperation. Factions and potential factions can go their own way, but they often choose to coordinate with one another instead.

6 Legislators

In this section, we focus on those endorsers who are also members of the U.S. House. The House provides useful context because it is home to formally organized caucuses.

As voluntary legislative member organizations, caucuses offer legislators an opportunity to collaborate with other legislators who share distinct policy or ideological priorities. Importantly, the caucus structure operates outside of the purview of House leadership, making it an ideal place for legislators to organize as dissenting groups or factions. Because of this, caucuses offer intra-party groups a means of getting what they want from their party since a united caucus of multiple legislators is more powerful than multiple legislators working alone. This feature also makes caucuses an ideal vehicle for intra-party factions.

Whatever the subject matter, House caucuses facilitate intra-party collective action. Any factions in Congress will likely be housed within caucuses (Bloch Rubin 2017; Clarke 2020; Blum 2020). And since these caucuses have formal membership, we know which factions the members in our data might be in. If our communities do map onto party factions, we would expect to see an overlap between certain caucuses and our communities.

There is evidence that Sanders' appeal is distinct, but notably, Donald Trump was the second choice of many activists, regardless of their first choice.

6.1 How Caucuses Overlap with Factions

Any group of legislators with a shared interest can form a caucus. Some of these are recreational (e.g., the Congressional Bike Caucus, which brings together cycling enthusiasts), others represent an identity group (e.g., the Congressional Black Caucus), while still others are formed around an ideological vision for the party (e.g., the Blue Dog Democrats, the Wednesday Group). As of 2023, the U.S. House is home to 376 official caucuses (Saksa 2023).[21]

Why join a caucus? The literature identifies three possible incentives. The first is social. Regardless of the topic, caucuses facilitate and solidify social connections (Victor 2009; Ringe and Victor 2012). The second involves signaling. Members might join an ideological caucus to send a signal to donors about their ideological proclivities (Gaynor 2022). The final incentive maps most closely maps onto our research question. An intra-party coalition with a perspective that is distinct from that of their party's leadership, or that is not consistently represented in their party's legislative efforts, has the best chance of affecting policy outcomes if they bind together (Bloch Rubin 2017, Seo and Theriault 2012).

In this sense, ideological and certain identity-based caucuses are a type of sub-party organization that closely maps onto our idea of factions. In this section, we look for overlaps between these caucuses and the communities we find. If they match, then those communities are probably representing the factions. If the communities combine many of these caucuses together, particularly caucuses that would seem to disagree with one another, then they are probably showing the cooperating behavior we've been describing.

This method has some limitations due to data coverage. Some of our communities have few members in Congress (especially the smaller communities). Our caucus data coverage largely begins with the 103rd Congress, in 1993–1994. This leaves us without caucus data for endorsers who served in Congress before that time, most of whom are in the Cold War and Reagan-Era communities. The results we obtain in these analyses tell us about the community/caucus overlap only for those communities with high data coverage but are less useful for the low data coverage communities.

---

[21] Caucuses are more commonly associated with the U.S. House, although Senators can technically join caucuses. Given the smaller size of the U.S. Senate and chamber rules that allow individual Senators more input over daily policy decisions, they have less need of alternative outlets for discussion and collaboration than do their colleagues in the House.

6.2 Caucus Data

Our caucus membership data come from one of the leading scholars on congressional caucuses, Jennifer Nicoll Victor (2023). Victor has compiled the most comprehensive database to date of caucus membership, ranging from the 103rd through the 116th Congresses (1993 to 2021). Victor's database includes membership information for all caucuses registered with the House Committee on Administration in that period. This overlaps a large part of our data, but not all of it. For members who served before the 103rd Congress, we checked our endorser list against membership lists of the Conservative Democratic Forum (CDF), early Blue Dog Democrats, and the Republican Study Committee from Bloch Rubin (2017). This process identified ten Democratic endorsers who were also members of the CDF.

In total, 1,116 unique caucuses were active between 1993 and 2021.[22] From this list, we selected those caucuses that map onto potential factions with the following three criteria.

1. They must be partisan caucuses, those for which membership is consistently from one party. Most bipartisan caucuses are not factions. They might focus on a specific contemporary policy issue (e.g., the Iraq War), or represent a specific delegation (e.g., the California Republican Delegation, the Democratic Sophomore Class of the 115th Congress).
2. They must line up with an identifiable faction or identity group in the party. Identity groups may or may not reflect factions themselves. However, at least in the Democratic Party, strong identity groups represent distinct interests in the party and mobilize in different ways. It is possible that certain identity groups are more integral to some communities than others.
3. They must persist across multiple sessions of Congress.

By these criteria, we find nine Democratic caucuses and twelve Republican caucuses. Many of the Republican caucuses had overlapping missions but existed at different points in time.

6.2.1 Democratic Factional Caucuses

Table 9 shows the Democratic caucuses of interest, including the number of endorsers in the caucus, sessions the caucus was active (not just the sessions for which we have data), and the intra-party division with which each caucus corresponds.

---

[22] Most of these caucuses were only active for a couple of sessions of Congress – 38 percent were active for one to two sessions, 72 percent for one to five, and only 1.8 percent were active for all 14 sessions in our data.

Table 9 Factional Democratic caucuses in the U.S. House.

Caucus	Endorsers	Sessions	Focus
New Democrat Coalition	83	105th–	Fiscally moderate, socially liberal
Congressional Progressive Caucus	79	102nd–	Fiscally and socially liberal
Congressional Black Caucus	69	92nd–	Identity group
Congressional Equality Caucus	57	114th–	LGBTQ+ identity group
Congressional Labor and Working Families Caucus	55	108th–	Labor interests
Congressional Hispanic Caucus	53	94th–	Identity group
Congressional Asian and Pacific Americans Caucus	49	104th–	Identity group
Blue Dog Coalition	38	104th–	Centrist
Conservative Democratic Forum	10	96th–97th	Southern conservatives

With two exceptions, these caucuses had a decades-long presence in the party. The Congressional Equality Caucus (formerly the Congressional LGBTQ Equality Caucus) is more recent, forming in 2015. This caucus nevertheless meets our requirement for a caucus representing a core identity group in the party.

The other exception is the CDF, one of several that represented the interests of conservative Southern Democrats within the Democratic Party. Predecessors include a Southern Democrat organizational apparatus, though not officially a caucus. These interests, or what remained of them in the party, were eventually taken up by the Blue Dog Coalition (Bloch Rubin 2017). We include the CDF because it is the only one of these caucuses for which a membership list is both obtainable and overlaps with the start of our endorsement data (1972). This makes the CDF the closest approximation we have of this faction in the early period of our data.

These nine caucuses represent the most likely intra-party divisions in the Democratic Party in the last thirty years, at least as they appear in the U.S. House.[23] The New Democrat Coalition, Progressive Caucus, Blue Dog Coalition, and CDF all represent different flavors of the Democratic Party,

---

[23] As with the conservative Democratic caucuses before 1993, we do not have a membership list for the Democratic Study Group, a prominent liberal caucus that existed from 1959–1993.

with divergent stances on social and economic policies. The Congressional Black Caucus, Hispanic Caucus, and Asian and Pacific Americans Caucus represent ethnic voting blocks in the party. The Equality Caucus represents LGBTQ interests, and the Labor and Working Families Caucus furthers the interests of organized labor.

6.2.2 Republican Factional Caucuses

The Republican landscape of factional caucuses is more complicated than the Democratic one. The Republicans tend to have multiple caucuses that map onto the same intra-party group, separated by time (e.g., the Wednesday Group gave way to the Republican Main Street Caucus). We identify four general groups of Republican factions: Tea Party Republicans, moderates/centrists, religious conservatives, and traditional conservatives. In narrowing down the caucuses of interest, we selected the caucuses for each possible faction that had the largest membership and/or persisted for the longest period[s] of time.

Table 10 lists these caucuses, again with the number of network members in that caucus, its active time frame, and its focus.

Unlike the Democratic caucuses of interest, which tended to have longer lifespans and often represented identity groups, the Republican caucuses crop up in clusters and map onto ideological camps in the party more so than onto identity groups.

The three earlier caucuses dovetail with the divisions in the party in the 1970s and 1980s. The Republican Study Committee represented and still represents traditional, Reagan-style conservatism. The Conservative Opportunity Society was the locus of Newt Gingrich's strategic efforts to foster a new Republican majority and became an important vehicle in the early 1990s Republican governance strategy, including the Contract with America. The Wednesday Group anchored the centrist end of the Republican Party.

After the Republicans seized majority control of the House in 1994, they formed several new caucuses. The Republican Main Street Caucus became a large centrist presence, the Tuesday Group formed to directly oppose the Conservative Opportunity Society's focus on the retrenchment of the welfare state, and the Mainstream Conservative Alliance formed to advocate for bipartisan and centrist solutions. The 1990s also saw the formation of several caucuses related to specific issues and/or groups in this period, including the Renewal Alliance, which advocated for faith-based alternatives to government welfare programs.

During the Bush Era in the early 2000s, religious conservatives formed the Prayer Caucus and the Values Action Caucus, and libertarians began meeting as

Table 10 Factional Republican caucuses in the U.S. House.

Caucus	N endorsers	Sessions	Focus
Republican Study Committee	46	93rd–	Traditional conservatism
Republican Main Street Caucus	32	105th–	Centrist
Prayer Caucus	18	110th–	Christian traditionalism
Conservative Opportunity Society	14	97th–115th	Strategy, anti-welfare
Tuesday Group	13	105th–	Moderate
Mainstream Conservative Alliance	12	104th–106th	Bipartisan centrists
Renewal Alliance	12	105th–107th	Charity-based solutions to poverty
Wednesday Group	11	88th–110th	Liberal Republican
House Freedom Caucus	6	114th–	Tea Party
Liberty Caucus	5	108th–	Tea Party/libertarian
Tea Party Caucus	4	113th–115th	Tea Party
Values Action Caucus	4	108th–	Christian values

part of the Liberty Caucus. Following the rise of the Tea Party in the 2010s, two more caucuses emerged: the Tea Party and the House Freedom Caucuses.

Taken together, Republican caucuses present a more complex picture than their Democratic counterparts. The Republican Main Street Caucus, Tuesday Group, Mainstream Conservative Alliance, and the Wednesday Group all map onto a possible centrist group or faction in the party. The Prayer Caucus, Renewal Alliance, and Values Action Caucus together represent the interests of conservative Christians. The Republican Study Group and the Conservative Opportunity Society both represent a more traditional vision of conservatism but differ both in terms of strategy (the latter being more electorally focused) and longevity (the former persisting longer). Finally, the Liberty, Tea Party, and House Freedom Caucuses all represent the interests of a Tea Party-style faction, members of which galvanized around the latter caucus in the late 2010s. Because of these overlaps, our analysis will evaluate the Republican caucuses both individually and grouped together with similar caucuses.

6.3 Members of Congress among the Endorsers

The analysis in this section focuses on endorsement network members who also served in Congress. Of the 873 endorsers in the Democratic network, that is a little over a third (223). Of the 422 Republican endorsers, the number is a little over half (227). Table 11 lists the number and proportion of endorsers from each community who served in Congress, as well as the number who were members of one of our caucuses of interest.

As noted earlier, congressional membership is not evenly distributed across endorser communities. For the Democrats, the two candidate-centered communities have dramatically fewer members in Congress than the establishment communities. The Progressives only have two members.

For the Republicans, a sizable proportion of establishment community members also served in Congress. This was even true in the smallest of the establishment communities, the Old Guard, where nearly 70 percent of endorsers served in Congress. The East Coast Republicans follow the trend of the non-establishment Democratic communities, with a lower number and proportion of members in Congress. The Mavericks lived up to their name. Despite their smaller numbers, a quarter of that community served in Congress.

Table 11 Endorsers from each community who ever served in Congress and who were members of a factional caucus in our data.

Community	N in Congress	Prop. in Congress	N in Caucuses
Democratic endorsers			
Cold War Establishment	124	45.9	47
Modern Establishment	146	33.2	100
Edwards Backers	16	12.7	14
Progressives	2	5.4	2
Republican endorsers			
Reagan-Era Establishment	30	46.9	2
Bush-Era Establishment	104	59.4	44
Post-Bush Establishment	25	35.7	22
Old Guard	23	69.7	12
East Coast Republicans	4	12.9	2
Mavericks	12	24.5	9

The analysis is also focused on the later time period in our data. Our endorsements date back to 1972, but our caucus data do not begin until 1993. We are unable to capture caucus membership for endorsers who retired from Congress before 1993. This primarily affects the Cold War and Reagan-Era Establishment communities.

The remaining communities, however, have a decent level of overlap between the total number of endorsers in Congress and the number who joined one of our caucuses of interest.

6.4 Divisions within Congress: Caucuses

Based on our theoretical framework, we expect two patterns in how our network communities overlap with factional congressional caucuses.

First, while our data coverage is weaker for the non-establishment communities we do have some expectations for them. These communities might overlap distinctly with some caucuses and exclude others. This would provide evidence that these communities represent factions, as well as a richer characterization of the types of factions they represent.

Second, we expect the establishment to unite different factions and other subgroups. So, our establishment communities ought to draw from multiple factional caucuses. This expectation can be evaluated more clearly than the first, especially for the more recent establishment communities where we have greater overlap with the caucus data. We thus focus on these communities.

In both parties, if the establishment communities really are coalitions – of groups and of factions – then we should expect their endorsers to join a variety of ideological and identity-based caucuses (e.g., the Democratic Modern Establishment should include endorsers from the Progressive Caucus, the Congressional Black Caucus, and the New Democrat Coalition). It is also possible, however, that the many Republican establishment communities will have distinct patterns, suggesting they reveal a cleavage among those backing establishment candidates.

The caucuses in our data have existed for multiple sessions of Congress, some for longer than others. The membership for each caucus shifts every two years, as members retire and/or are replaced by other representatives. We combine membership for each caucus across all available sessions. Any endorser who was a member of a caucus at any time is coded as in the caucus, and any endorser who never joined this caucus is coded as not in it.

Our figures show the proportion of the endorsers in each caucus from each community. Our analyses can thus be interpreted as showing the relative importance of each community in each caucus. Communities with fewer members of Congress will make up smaller proportions of each caucus, but these differences will be less pronounced than if we used counts. In using the number of endorsers in each caucus as the denominator, we can gain purchase on the possibility that those party members who make presidential endorsements are also members of durable factions.

6.4.1 Democratic Caucus–Community Overlaps

Figure 26 shows the proportion of Democratic endorsers by community in each of the nine caucuses of interest.

We begin with the Cold War Establishment. Although many of these endorsers served in Congress before the caucus data coverage began, forty-seven endorsers are members of at least one of these nine caucuses. These endorsers have a presence in all nine caucuses. They make up a definite majority of the

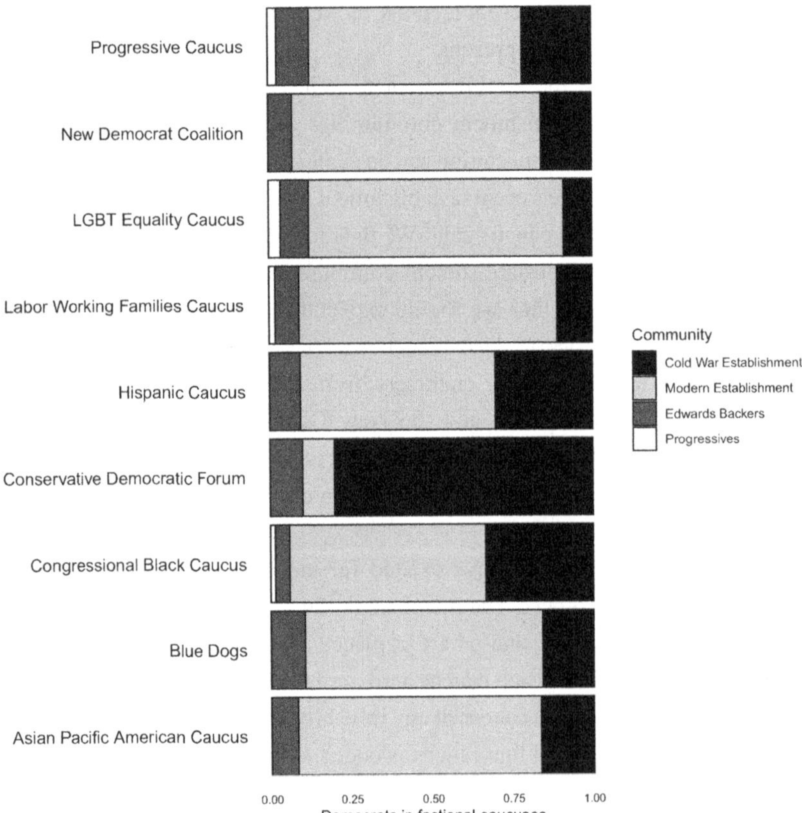

Figure 26 Establishment Democratic endorser communities have members across factional caucuses.

CDF, which is what we would expect based on the time frame in which both these endorsers and that caucus were active. They also make up about a third of the endorsers in the Hispanic and Congressional Black Caucuses, with lower proportions of members in more recently formed caucuses like the LGBT Equality and the Labor and Working Families Caucuses.

Of members of the Modern Establishment, for whom we have the best data coverage, 100 endorsers are members of one of these caucuses and also have representation across all nine caucuses. Members of this community represent every possible faction in the Democratic Party (some even were part of the CDF). This is in line with what we have come to expect from an establishment community.

The final two caucuses have fewer members of Congress, and fewer still who are in one of these caucuses (two Progressives and twelve Edwards Backers are represented). The two Progressives in Congress, Keith Ellison (D-MN) and Peter Welch (D-VT), are both members of the LGBT Equality and Progressive Caucuses. One member each is in the Labor and Working Families Caucus and the Congressional Black Caucus. The Edwards Backers are distributed relatively evenly across all nine caucuses (except for the Congressional Black Caucus, where there are fewer).

In general, and despite variation in data coverage, these findings suggest that a narrative of cooperation is the most appropriate for the Democratic endorsers who served in Congress. Both establishment communities include endorsers who represent distinct groups in the party, from Progressives to Black Americans. These groups seem to have made the determination that, at least when it comes to presidential nominations, cooperating as part of a large and cohesive establishment is more important than going it alone. The small number of Progressives and Edwards Backers in Congress makes it difficult to draw conclusions about these communities. The lack of representation in Congress for these communities is evidence itself that they are distinct, but we cannot say in what way.

6.4.2 Republican Caucus–Community Overlaps

As we noted earlier, we categorize the Republican caucuses into four groups: Tea Party-style, religious, moderate, and traditional. Each of these groups represents a different part of the party, which might be the basis of a faction. We break down members by caucus grouping in Figure 27.

The two communities with the most endorser–caucus overlaps are the Bush-Era and Post-Bush Establishment. As with the Democratic Modern Establishment, members of the Republican Establishment communities are also members of most

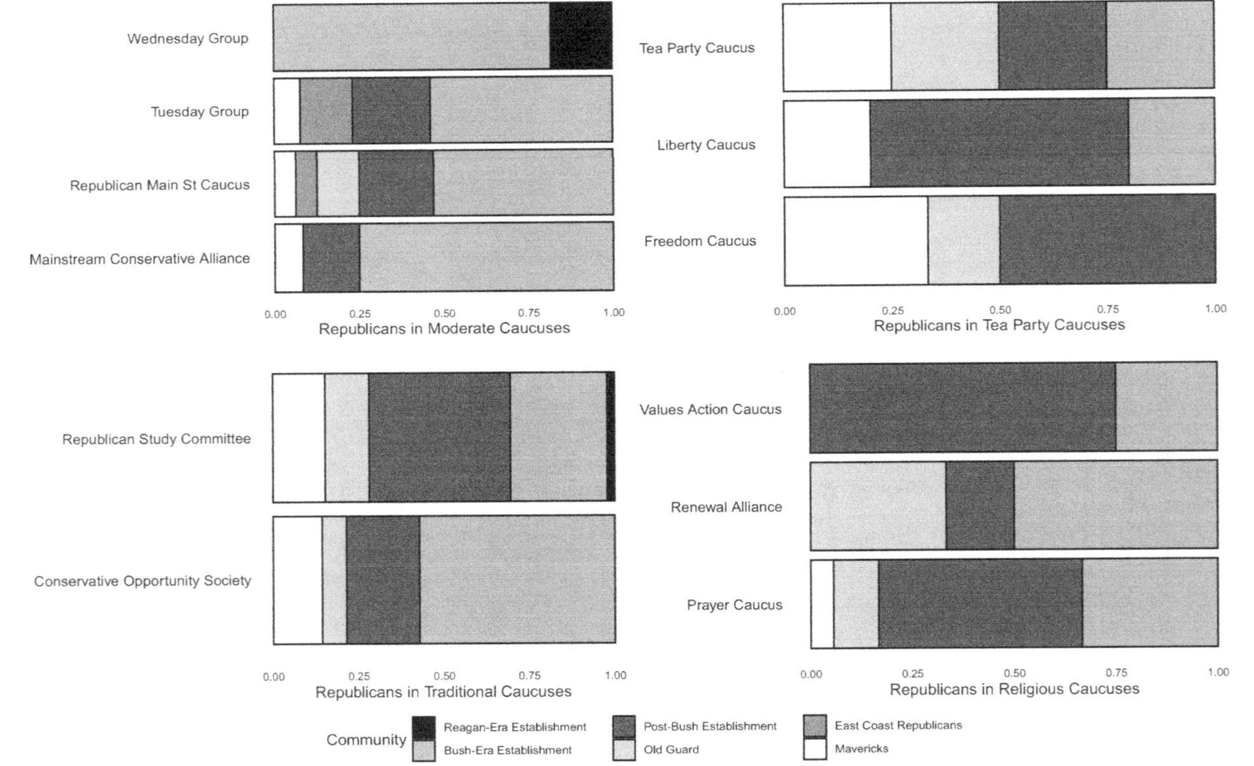

Figure 27 Shaded bars show the proportion of Republican endorsers from each community in each caucus. Caucuses are grouped by the faction with which they generally align.

caucuses (except for the Freedom Caucus for the Bush-Era Establishment and the Wednesday Group for the Post-Bush Establishment). So, again, these establishment communities seem to be uniting many factions in Congress. We suspect the same would be true of the Reagan-Era Establishment if we had data on caucuses from that period.

As with the Democrats, our two factional caucuses are not so broadly represented. Again, this impedes our ability to draw substantive conclusions about these communities. From the data we have, the Mavericks have considerable overlap with the Tea Party caucuses, despite John McCain's sometimes quite public disagreements with that wing of the party. The Mavericks are absent from the religious caucuses. That is consistent with McCain's opposition to the religious right. As noted before, this group seems largely driven by their support for McCain as a person, but if there is anything more substantive revealed here, it is the lack of support from the religious right.

The East Coast Republicans, for whom we also have scant data coverage, only overlap with the moderate caucuses. They have no Tea Party-adjacent caucus members, no religious caucus members, and no traditional conservative members. The East Coast Republicans are, as we have noted before, a more moderate faction that draws from a declining tradition in the party. These results, though spotty, are in line with that interpretation.

We also have an interesting pattern with the Old Guard. We have called them an establishment faction because they support establishment candidates. But as we have noted before, they are a little different from the rest of the establishment. They are a little more conservative, more concentrated in national office, and their leaders include key donors. Now, we see them as relatively unrepresented among the moderate caucuses.

This suggests perhaps a slightly different picture for the Republican Party as a whole. The bulk of the party in recent decades has been positioned between a conservative wing and a moderate wing. But the very conservative wing is in the ascendant. The Old Guard and the Post-Bush Establishment are the most conservative communities, and they mostly endorsed the eventual winners.

6.5 Evidence of Factionalism?

The findings from this section, where we have isolated our analysis to endorsers who also served in Congress, shed light on an important phenomenon. We have argued that presidential nominations will blur the effects of factions, as they cooperate. This is not because there are no factions, but because factions often cooperate with the "establishment." Indeed, the establishment is, in some ways, the result of factional cooperation.

In mapping our endorsers onto factional caucuses, we find evidence of this phenomenon. While a few of the smaller communities seem to have their own ideological quirks, the establishment communities are home to endorsers who represent a variety of factional groups. While these endorsers might represent different interests in arenas like Congress, they cooperate more often than not when it comes to presidential nominations.

7 Implications

Every four years, leading figures in one or both major parties throw their hats in the ring to be considered as their party's nominee for president. When they do, the rest of the party can assess the candidates and line up behind one of them.

In making an endorsement, a public statement of support, party elites are taking sides in what can be described as a battle for the future of the party. Which side wins is determined by those voters who participate in the primaries and caucuses, but the party elites are drawing the battle lines.

The nomination can be described this way, emphasizing the conflict and drama. But we think this description misses something important. It treats presidential nominations like a tournament, with candidates competing in their party's contest, and then the winners facing off in the championship game.

Yet intra-party conflict is different than inter-party conflict. Nominations are an opportunity to let internal differences rise to the surface, but the parties' interest in cohesion remains. Unlike in a tournament, the winning candidate does not go on to face the other party alone. To be successful in the general election, they must garner support from the factions they defeated in the primary. Party leaders understand this, and they act to create a consensus candidate, even in the context of an intra-party fight.

We set out to see if we could find evidence of the factional conflict that is under the surface of a presidential nomination fight. But we also expected to find evidence of coordination and cooperation.

We think we have found both.

In each party, we find a set of communities that are well-described as the establishment. They are big-tent communities, embracing insider candidates. Among Democrats, there are two such communities; one giving way to the other over time. Among Republicans, there are four. Three of them replace one another in succession. And a fourth is a conservative, national group of well-connected politicos.

In each party, we also find a set of communities that look to us like factions. They are distinct in various meaningful ways from the establishment communities. They tend to be short-lived, supporting one or a small set of candidates. The candidates they back rarely win the nomination.

It would be hard to understand these data without accounting for both types of party behavior. The communities formed through shared endorsement patterns are not the result of actors having different preferences. On the contrary, the establishment communities are coalitions of actors with different preferences. Rather, these communities are the result of actors having different strategies. Some cooperate and become part of the nomination establishment, and some do not.

We draw three important implications from our analysis. First, intra-party factional conflict is different from inter-party conflict. Second, network analysis is a powerful tool for understanding factions, but it must be guided by theory. Finally, factions are not new, but they may play a larger role in future U.S. politics than they have in the last several decades.

7.1 Intra-party Politics Is Different than Inter-party Politics

The way U.S. parties choose their presidential candidates encourages both voters and candidates to view the nomination as a mini version of the final event. People vote for the prospective nominees, and then they vote for the prospective president.

But if we look at the process from the point of view of the rest of the politicians who are not running for office, the difference between the two stages is more evident.

Much of the value of the nomination comes from the unity that the whole party brings to the general election. Thus, fights over the nomination are about two things: different visions of the party, and different estimations of the importance of party unity.

Different actors will balance these different needs differently, leading to the two strategies we think we have detected in the endorsement data. Some join to reshape the party, forming what we observe as the establishment. Others try to redirect the party more forcefully.

7.2 Network Methods Can Reveal Factions

The questions we have raised here cannot be easily answered if we treat endorsers as atomistic actors. We also can't just summarize their behavior by looking at who they endorse the most. What matters is the endorsers' relationship to one another.

Social network analysis is an ideal way to look at patterns in relationships. Community detection, centrality, and other network methods provide data-driven answers to questions about the outlines of intra-party groups, and the relative connectedness of different actors in the party. But it is not without its limitations. Like all methods, the patterns we observe need to be interpreted. Two people who endorse the same candidate might have a different relationship than two people who interact directly.

To do so, we leverage our theories about what kinds of behavior we would expect to see from factional actors and collaborating actors. With those theories in mind, we expect two different patterns, which we do find.

7.3 A Factional Future?

In both parties, we find evidence of several factions. Most of those factions arise in the latter half of our period of data coverage (e.g., after the year 2000). Does that mean factions are becoming more common?

They might be.

One argument for why party leaders have been less influential in recent contests (Cohen et al. 2016) is that the parties have more internal divisions, which are harder to overcome. Similarly, the U.S. House has for decades been able to choose a speaker without the chaos of recent attempts.

At the same time, internal divisions are not new. In many ways, the current Democratic and Republican parties are far more homogeneous today than they were a half-century ago.

What is different is the rising popularity of certain factional strategies within the parties. It is not simply that there are disagreements. It is that there are disagreements over how to manage those disagreements. Cooperation is far from gone, but those who wish to cooperate must share the parties with factional agents who turn to insurgent strategies.

Those who want to see more intra-party coordination might take comfort in our results, which show the party coming together despite the lack of an institutional mechanism forcing them. In some ways, it's an impressive accomplishment, given the way the rules are stacked against such cooperation. And if we believe *The Party Decides* that such an agreement can help select a nominee, such cooperation might be encouraging.

We have little evidence that the candidate they settle on in this informal arena is the best candidate, or that the current process is not flawed just because party leaders are able to coordinate. What we do show, however, is despite the perception of "civil wars" in the parties, the sides are not always engaged in battle.

References

Adkins, Randall E., and Andrew Dowdle. 2005. "Do Early Birds Get the Worm? Improving Timeliness of Presidential Nomination Forecasts." *Presidential Studies Quarterly* 35(4):646–660.

Aldrich, John. 1995. *Why Parties? The Origin and Transformation of Political Parties in America*. University of Chicago Press.

Allen, Jonathan, and Amie Parnes. 2021. *Lucky: How Joe Biden Barely Won the Presidency*. Crown.

Antle, W. James III. 2019. "How 'Democrats Fall in Love, Republicans Fall in Line' Got Flipped upside down." *The Week*. June 19. https://theweek.com/articles/846998/how-democrats-fall-love-republicans-fall-line-got-flipped-upside-down.

Arceneaux, Michael. 2016. "Bernie Sanders Still Says Class Is More Important than Race: He Is Still Wrong." *The Guardian*. November 22. www.theguardian.com/commentisfree/2016/nov/22/bernie-sanders-identity-politics-class-race-debate.

Azari, Julia. 2023. "Weak Parties, Strong Partisanship." In *The Making of the Presidential Candidates 2024*, eds. Jonathan Bernstein and Casey B. K. Dominguez. Rowman Littlefield. Chapter 3.

Bacon Jr., Perry. 2020. "Why Warren Couldn't Win." *FiveThirtyEight*. March 5. https://fivethirtyeight.com/features/why-warren-couldnt-win/#:~:text=So%20whatever%20her%20campaign%20tactics,voters%20are%20obsessed%20with%20this.

Bartolini, Stefano, and Peter Mair. 1990. *Identity, Competition, and Electoral Availability: The Stabilisation of European Electorates 1885–1985*. Cambridge University Press.

Bawn, Kathleen. 1999. "Constructing 'Us': Ideology, Coalition Politics, and False Consciousness." *American Journal of Political Science* 43(2):303–334.

Bawn, Kathy, Marty Cohen, David Karol et al. 2012. "A Theory of Political Parties: Groups, Policy Demands and Nominations in American Politics." *Perspectives on Politics* 10(3):571–597.

Beck, Paul Allen. 1984. "Young vs. Old in 1984: Generations and Life Stages in Presidential Nomination Politics." *PS: Political Science & Politics* 17 (3):515–524.

Berkowitz, Peter. 2015. "Can Trump, Cruz Win over GOP's 'Four Factions'?" *Real Clear Politics*. December 10. www.realclearpolitics.com/articles/2015/12/10/can_trump_cruz_win_over_gops_four_factions_128987.html.

Bernstein, Jonathan. 2019. "The Expanded Party's Influence." In *The Making of the Presidential Candidates 2020*, eds. Jonathan Bernstein and Casey B. K. Dominguez. Rowman & Littlefield.

Bernstein, Jonathan. 2023. "The Parties and Party Nominations." In *The Making of the Presidential Candidates 2024*, eds. Jonathan Bernstein and Casey B. K. Dominguez. Rowman & Littlefield. Chapter 2.

Biden, Joe. 2020. *Joe Biden Outlines New Steps to Ease Economic Burden on Working People*. April 9. https://medium.com/@JoeBiden/joe-biden-out lines-new-steps-to-ease-economic-burden-on-working-people-e3e121037322.

Bloch Rubin, Ruth. 2017. *Building the Bloc: Intraparty Organization in the U.S. Congress*. Cambridge University Press.

Blum, Rachel. 2020. *How the Tea Party Captured the GOP: Insurgent Factions in American Politics*. University of Chicago Press.

Blum, Rachel. In press. *The Asymmetry of Movement-Factions in the Democratic and Republican Parties*. In *Placing Parties in American Political Development*, eds. Adam Hilton and Jessica Hejny. University of Pennsylvania Press.

Blum, Rachel, and Michael Cowburn. 2024. "How Local Factions Pressure Parties: Activist Groups and Primary Contests in the Tea Party Era." *British Journal of Political Science* 54(1):788–109.

Bonica, Adam. 2023. *Database on Ideology, Money in Politics, and Elections: Public Version 3.1* [Computer file]. Stanford University Libraries. https://data.stanford.edu/dime.

Borgatti, Stephen P., Martin G. Everett. 1997. "Network Analysis of 2-Mode Data." *Social Networks* 19:243–269.

Brandes, Ulrik, Stephen P. Borgatti, and Linton C. Freeman. 2016. "Maintaining the Duality of Closeness and Betweenness Centrality." *Social Networks* 44:153–159.

Bump, Philip. 2015. "The 2016 GOP Presidential Race, Broken Down into 5 'Lanes'." *The Washington Post*. www.washingtonpost.com/news/the-fix/wp/2015/03/25/breaking-down-the-lanes-theory-of-the-2016-republican-field/.

Cantor, Eric, Kevin McCarthy, and Paul Ryan. 2010. *Young Guns: A New Generation of Conservative Leaders*. Simon and Schuster.

Christakis, Nicholas A., and James H. Fowler. 2007. "The Spread of Obesity in a Large Social Network over 32 years." *New England Journal of Medicine* 357(4):370–379.

Christakis, Nicholas A., and James H. Fowler. 2008. "The Collective Dynamics of Smoking in a Large Social Network." *New England Journal of Medicine* 358(21):2249–2258.

Christakis, Nicholas A., and James H. Fowler. 2009. *Connected: The Surprising Power of our Social Networks and How They Shape our Lives*. Little, Brown, and Spark.

Clark, William Roberts, and Matt Golder. 2006. "Rehabilitating Duverger's Theory: Testing the Mechanical and Strategic Modifying Effects of Electoral Laws." *Comparative Political Studies* 39(6):679–708.

Clarke, Andrew J. 2020. "Party Sub-Brands and American Party Factions." *American Journal of Political Science* 64(3):452–470.

Cohen-Cole, Ethan, and Jason M. Fletcher. 2008a. "Detecting Implausible Social Network Effects in Acne, Height, and Headaches: Longitudinal Analysis." *British Medical Journal* 337.

Cohen-Cole, Ethan, and Jason M. Fletcher. 2008b. "Is Obesity Contagious? Social Networks vs. Environmental Factors in the Obesity Epidemic." *Journal of Health Economics* 27(5):1382–1387.

Cohen, Marty. 2019. *Moral Victories in the Battle for Congress*. University of Pennsylvania Press.

Cohen, Marty, David Karol, Hans Noel, and John Zaller. 2007. "The Invisible Primary in Presidential Nominations, 1980–2004." In *The Making of the Presidential Candidates 2008*, ed. Willam G. Mayer. Rowman and Littlefield.

Cohen, Marty, David Karol, Hans Noel, and John Zaller. 2008. *The Party Decides: Presidential Nominations before and after Reform*. University of Chicago Press.

Cohen, Marty, David Karol, Hans Noel, and John Zaller. 2016. "Party versus Faction in the Reformed Presidential Nominating System." *PS: Political Science and Politics* 43(4): 701–708.

Conroy, Meredith, and Ciera Hammond. 2023. "How Gender Shapes Presidential Primary Campaigns and Elections." In *The Making of the Presidential Candidates 2024*, eds. Jonathan Bernstein and Casey B. K. Dominguez. Rowman & Littlefield. Chapter 7.

Dann, Carrie 2015. "Bernie Sanders: Racism, Economic Inequality are 'Parallel Problems,'" *NBC News*. July 26. www.nbcnews.com/meet-the-press/bernie-sanders-racism-economic-inequality-are-parallel-problems-n398581.

Devega, Chauncey. 2016. "There Is No GOP Establishment Lane! There Is a Proto-fascist, a Christian Theocrat, and an Ayn Rand Neoliberal." *Salon*.

DiSalvo, Daniel. 2012. *Engines of Change*. Oxford University Press.

Dominguez, Casey, and Jonathan Bernstein. 2003. "Candidates and Candidacies in the Expanded Party." *PS: Political Science and Politics* 36(2):165–169.

Dowdle, Andrew J., Randall E. Adkins, and Wayne Steger. 2009. "The Viability Primary: Modeling Candidate Support before the Primaries." *Political Research Quarterly* 61(1):77–91.

Duck-Mayr, J. Brandon, and Jacob Montgomery. 2023. "Ends against the Middle: Measuring Latent Traits when Opposites Respond the Same Way for Antithetical Reasons." *Political Analysis*. 31(4):606–625.

Dunleavy, Patrick. 2012. "Duverger's Law Is a Dead Parrot. Outside the USA, First-Past-the-Post Voting Has No Tendency At All to Produce Two Party Politics." *London School of Economics* blog. https://blogs.lse.ac.uk/politic sandpolicy/duvergers-law-dead-parrot-dunleavy/ (June 18, 2012).

Ellen, Jonathan M. 2009. "Social Networks Research and Challenges to Causal Inference." *Journal of Adolescent Health* 45(2):109–110.

Ellis, Christopher, and James A. Stimson. 2012. *Ideology in America*. Cambridge University Press.

Emanuele, Vincenzo, and Alessandro Chiaramonte. 2019. "Explaining the Impact of New Parties in the Western European Party Systems." *Journal of Elections, Public Opinion and Parties* 29(4): 490–510.

FiveThirtyEight. 2020. "The 2020 Endorsement Primary." *Fivethirtyeight.com*. April 8. https://projects.fivethirtyeight.com/2020-endorsements/democratic-primary/.

FiveThirtyEight. 2024. "Which 2024 Republican Presidential Candidate Has the Most Endorsements?" *Fivethirtyeight.com*. March 6, 2024. https://pro jects.fivethirtyeight.com/2024-election-endorsements/.

Fowler, James H., and Nicholas A. Christakis. 2008. "Dynamic Spread of Happiness in a Large Social Network: Longitudinal Analysis over 20 Years in the Framingham Heart Study." *British Medical Journal* 337(a2338):337–346. https://doi.org/10.1136/bmj.a2338.

Fowler, James H., and Nicholas A. Christakis. 2010. "Cooperative Behavior Cascades in Human Social Networks." *Proceedings of the National Academy of Sciences* 107(12):5334–5338.

Fowler, James H., Michael T. Heaney, David W. Nickerson, John F. Padgett, and Betsy Sinclair. 2011. "Causality in Political Networks." *American Politics Research* 39(2):437–480.

Gaynor, SoRelle Wyckoff. 2022. "The (Financial) Ties That Bind: Social Networks of Intraparty Caucuses." *Legislative Studies Quarterly* 47(4):885–920.

Grossmann, Matt, and David A. Hopkins. 2016. *Asymmetric Politics: Ideological Republicans and Group Interest Democrats*. Oxford University Press.

Halperin, Mark, and John Heilemann. 2013. *Double Down: Game Change 2012*. Penguin Press.

Hare, Christopher, and Keith T. Poole. 2014. "The Polarization of Contemporary American Politics." *Polity* 46(3):411–429.

Hopkins, Dan. 2016. "Clinton Voters Like Obama More Than Sanders Supporters Do." *FiveThirtyEight*. March 7. https://fivethirtyeight.com/features/voters-who-like-obama-like-clinton/.

Hopkins, Daniel J., and Gall Sigler. 2024. "Not of Primary Concern: Stability, Ideology, and Vote Choice in U.S. Primaries, 2008–2024." Working Paper. https://papers.ssrn.com/sol3/papers.cfm?abstract_id=4733037.

Hopkins, Daniel J., and Hans Noel. 2022. "Trump and the Shifting Meaning of 'Conservative': Using Activists' Pairwise Comparisons to Measure Politicians' Perceived Ideologies." *American Political Science Review* 116(3):1133–1140.

Hussey, Wesley. 2008. "Coalition of Extremes: Ideology and Partisanship in the United States Congress, 1947–1998." *Ph.D. Dissertation, UCLA*.

ISU/Civiqs. 2020. "Iowa State University/Civiqs Poll." Iowa State University. www.news.iastate.edu/news/2020/01/29/caucuspoll.

Kamarck, Elaine. 2016. *Primary Politics: Everything You Need to Know about How America Nominates Its Presidential Candidates*. Brookings Institution Press.

Karol, David. 2009. *Party Position Change in American Politics: Coalition Management*. Cambridge University Press.

Kinnard, Meg. 2023. "Nikki Haley Argues Donald Trump Is Always Followed by 'Chaos' before a Large South Carolina Crowd," *Associated Press*. November 27. https://apnews.com/article/nikki-haley-2024-president-south-carolina-dcbbc177346d9b441b9ba9d50d755756#:~:text=Haley%20invoked%20her%20former%20boss%20saying%2C%20as%20she%20has%20before,follows%20him%2C%E2%80%9D%20Haley%20said.

Klein, Ezra. 2023. "Three Reasons the Republican Party Keeps Coming Apart at the Seams." *The New York Times*. January 15. www.nytimes.com/2023/01/15/opinion/mccarthy-republicans-coming-apart.html.

Knoke, David, and Tetiana Kostiuchenko. 2016. Power Structures of Policy Networks. In *The Oxford Handbook of Political Networks*, eds. Alexander H. Montgomery, Jennifer Nicoll Victor, and Mark Lubell. Oxford University Press.

Korecki, Natasha. 2020. "How Biden Engineered His Astonishing Comeback." *Politico*. March 2. www.politico.com/news/2020/03/02/centrists-biden-super-tuesday-bloomberg-118853.

Korecki, Natasha, and David Siders. 2020. "Sanders Sends Democratic Establishment into Panic Mode." *Politico*. February 23. www.politico.com/news/2020/02/23/sanders-democratic-establishment-panic-mode-117065.

Latapy, Matthieu, Clémence Magnien, and Nathalie Del Vecchio. 2008. "Basic Notions for the Analysis of Large Two-Mode Networks." *Social Networks* 30(1):31–48.

Lazer, David. 2011. "Networks in Political Science: Back to the Future." *PS: Political Science & Politics* 44(1):61–68.

Lee, Frances E. 2010. *Beyond Ideology: Politics, Principles, and Partisanship in the U. S. Senate*. University of Chicago Press.

Lelkes, Yphtach, and Paul M. Sniderman. 2016. "The Ideological Asymmetry of the American Party System." *British Journal of Political Science* 46(4):825–844.

Lupton, Robert N., William M. Myers, and Judd R. Thornton. 2017. "Party Animals: Asymmetric Ideological Constraint among Democratic and Republican Party Activists." *Political Research Quarterly* 70(4):889–904.

Martin, Jonathan, and Reid Epstein. 2019. "With the 2020 Democratic Field Set, Candidates Begin the Races within the Race." *The New York Times*. May 27. www.nytimes.com/2019/05/27/us/politics/2020-candi dates-iowa.html.

Mayer, William G. 1996. Forecasting Presidential Nominations. In *In Pursuit of the White House: How We Choose Our Presidential Nominees*, ed. William G. Mayer. Chatham House.

McLaughlin, Dan. 2019. "Five Lanes in the 2020 Democratic Field." *National Review*. March 14. www.nationalreview.com/2019/03/five-lanes-in-the-2020-democratic-field/.

McSweeney, Patrick. n.d. "Age Gaps in Party Member Evaluations of Political Parties and Leaders." *Working Paper*.

Mills, C. Wright. 1956. *The Power Elite*. Reprint, Oxford University Press, 2000.

Miroff, Bruce. 2009. *The Liberals' Moment: The McGovern Insurgency and the Identity Crisis of the Democratic Party*. University Press of Kansas.

Mitchell, Lincoln. 2011. "Republicans Aren't Falling in Line in 2012." *The Huffington Post*. April 12. www.huffpost.com/entry/republicans-arent-falling_b_847973.

Munger, Kevin. 2022. *Generation Gap: Why the Baby Boomers Still Dominate American Politics and Culture*. Columbia University Press.

Noel, Hans. 2013. *Political Ideologies and Political Parties in America*. Cambridge University Press.

Noel, Hans. 2016a. "Ideological Factions in the Republican and Democratic Parties." *The ANNALS of the American Academy of Political and Social Science* 667(1):166–188.

Noel, Hans. 2016b. "Why Can't the G.O.P. Stop Trump?" *The New York Times*. March 1. www.nytimes.com/2016/03/01/opinion/campaign-stops/why-cant-the-gop-stop-trump.html.

Noel, Hans. 2018. "The Activists Decide: The Preferences of Party Activists in the 2016 Presidential Nominations." *Journal of Elections, Public Opinion and Parties* 28(2):225–244.

Noel, Hans. n.d. Separating Ideology from Party in Roll Call Data.

Noel, Hans, and Brendan Nyhan. 2011. "The 'Unfriending' Problem: The Consequences of Homophily in Friendship Retention for Causal Estimates of Social Influence." *Social Networks* 33(3):211–218.

Norrander, Barbara. 1993. "Nomination Choices: Caucus and Primary Outcomes, 1976–1988." *American Journal of Political Science* 37:343–364.

Otterbein, Holly. 2019. "Bernie's Pollster Dishes on the Path to Beat Trump." *Politico*. February 19. www.politico.com/story/2019/02/19/bernie-sanders-campaign-2020-1173608.

Patty, John W., and Elizabeth Maggie Penn. 2016. Network Theory and Political Science. In *The Oxford Handbook of Political Networks*, eds. Alexander H. Montgomery, Jennifer Nicoll Victor, and Mark Lubell. Oxford University Press.

Peterson, David A. M. 2020. "The Dynamics of Iowa Democrats' Preferences." *Paper Presented at the 2020 University of Iowa, Iowa Caucus Conference.*

Polsby, Nelson. 1983. *Consequences of Party Reform*. Oxford University Press.

Pons, Pascal, and Matthieu Latapy. 2005. Computing Communities in Large Networks Using Random Walks. In *Computer and Information Sciences-ISCIS 2005*, eds. Pinar Yolum, Tunga Gungor, Fikret Gurgen, and Can Ozturan. Springer.

Poole, Keith, and Howard Rosenthal. 1997. *Congress: A Political-Economic History of Roll Call Voting*. Oxford University Press.

Poole, Keith T., and Howard Rosenthal. 1991. "Patterns of Congressional Voting." *American Journal of Political Science* 35(1):228–278.

Poole, Keith T., and Howard Rosenthal. 2007. *Ideology and Congress*. Transaction Publishers.

Ringe, Nils, and Jennifer Nicoll Victo. 2012. *Bridging the Information Gap: Legislative Member Organizations as Social Networks in the United States and the European Union," (with Christopher J. Carman)* University of Michigan Press.

Rios, Simón. 2016. "Bernie Sanders, in Boston: Democratic Party Needs To Focus On Working Class." *WBUR*. November 21. www.wbur.org/news/2016/11/21/bernie-sanders-berklee.

Rosenbluth, Frances, and Ian Shapiro. 2018. *Responsible Parties*: *Saving Democracy from Itself*. Yale University Press.

Saksa, Jim. 2023. "Estuaries? Pickleball? Rum? There's a Congressional Caucus for Practically Everything." *Roll Call*. Accessed: 2023–11–22.

Schattschneider, Elmer Eric. 1942. *Party Government*. Greenwood Press.

Schlozman, Daniel. 2016. *When Movements Anchor Parties*: *Electoral Alignments in American History*. Princeton University Press.

Schlozman, Daniel, and Sam Rosenfeld. 2024. *The Hollow Parties*: *The Many Pasts and Disordered Present of American Party Politics*. Princeton University Press.

Scholz, John T., Ramiro Berardo, and Brad Kile. 2008. "Do Networks Solve Collective Action Problems? Credibility, Search, and Collaboration." *The Journal of Politics* 70(2):393–406.

Schwartz, Thomas. 1989. *Why Parties?* Research memorandum.

Scott, Dylan. 2019. "The Competing Paths to the 2020 Democratic Presidential Nomination, Explained." *Vox*. June 21. www.vox.com/2019/6/21/18683892/2020-election-democratic-presidential-candidates-who-will-win.

Searles, Kathleen, and Patrick Rose. 2019. "How the News Media Cover and Shape the Nomination," In *The Making of the Presidential Candidates 2020*, eds. Jonathan Bernstein and Casey B. K. Dominguez. Rowman & Littlefield.

Seo, Jungkun, and Sean M. Theriault. 2012. "Moderate Caucuses in a Polarised US Congress." *The Journal of Legislative Studies* 18(2):203–221.

Shalizi, Cosma R., and Andrew C. Thomas. 2011. "Homophily and Contagion Are Generically Confounded in Observational Social Network Studies." *Sociological Methods and Research* 40:211–239.

Skinner, Richard M., Seth E. Masket, and David A. Dulio. 2012. "527 Committees and the Political Party Network." *American Politics Research* 40(1):60–84.

Steger, Wayne P. 2007. "Who Wins Presidential Nominations and Why: An Updated Forecast of the Presidential Primary Vote." *Presidential Research Quarterly* 60:91–97.

Sundquist, James L. 1983. *Dynamics of the Party System*: *Alignment and Realignment of Political Parties in the United States*. Brookings Institution.

Tarrow, Sidney. 2021. *Movements and Parties*: *Critical Connections in American Political Development*. Cambridge Studies in Contentious Politics Cambridge University Press.

Theriault, Sean. 2008. *Party Polarization in Congress*. Cambridge University Press.

Victor, Jennifer Nicoll. 2023. "Congressional Caucus Data: 103rd–116th Congresses." Provided by author. Accessed: 2023-06-07.

Victor, Jennifer Nicoll, and Nils Ringe. 2009. "The Social Utility of Informal Institutions: Caucuses as Networks in the 110th US House of Representatives." *American Politics Research* 37(5):742–766.

Wilson, Reid. 2016. "The Three Republican Lanes: Establishment, Values, Change." *Morning Consult*. February 20. https://morningconsult.com/2016/02/20/the-three-republican-lanes-establishment-values-change/.

Yang, Song, Scott Limbocker, Andrew J. Dowdle, Patrick A. Stewart, and Karen D. Sebold. 2013. "Party Cohesion in Presidential Races: Applying Social Network Theory to the Preprimary Multiple Donor Networks of 2004 and 2008." *Party Politics* 21(4):638–648.

Acknowledgments

This project was made possible through the data collection and cleaning efforts of many research assistants. We wish to extend our thanks to University of Oklahoma students Peter McLaughlin, Bennie Ashton, Sarina Rhinehart, Joy Rhodes, and Katie Kernal. We also thank Georgetown University students Jacob Livesay, Olivia Murray, Scott Romberg, Emily Ross, Lindsey Blechman, Susanna Blount, Margot Mather, Arianna Ashley Nassiri, Ryan Costley, Matthew Kahn, and others. In addition, earlier stages of this project greatly benefited from comments by Jennifer Victor, Seth Masket, David Karol, Liz Gerber, Vanessa Williamson, Suzanne Robbins, Richard Johnston, and other participants at political science workshops and conferences. We thank Dave Peterson, Daniel Hopkins, Gall Sigler, and Jennifer Victor for sharing data.

Cambridge Elements

American Politics

Frances E. Lee
Princeton University

Frances E. Lee is Professor of Politics at the Woodrow Wilson School of Princeton University. She is author of *Insecure Majorities: Congress and the Perpetual Campaign* (2016), *Beyond Ideology: Politics, Principles and Partisanship in the U.S. Senate* (2009), and coauthor of *Sizing Up the Senate: The Unequal Consequences of Equal Representation* (1999).

Advisory Board

Larry M. Bartels, *Vanderbilt University*
Marc Hetherington, *University of North Carolina at Chapel Hill*
Geoffrey C. Layman, *University of Notre Dame*
Suzanne Mettler, *Cornell University*
Hans Noel, *Georgetown University*
Eric Schickler, *University of California, Berkeley*
John Sides, *George Washington University*
Laura Stoker, *University of California, Berkeley*

About the Series

The Cambridge Elements Series in American Politics publishes authoritative contributions on American politics. Emphasizing works that address big, topical questions within the American political landscape, the series is open to all branches of the subfield and actively welcomes works that bridge subject domains. It publishes both original new research on topics likely to be of interest to a broad audience and state-of-the-art synthesis and reconsideration pieces that address salient questions and incorporate new data and cases to inform arguments.

Cambridge Elements $^{\equiv}$

American Politics

Elements in the Series

A full series listing is available at: www.cambridge.org/EAMP

Made in the USA
Monee, IL
07 July 2026

56552411R00066